Praise for *Habits for Our Holiness*

Thanks to Philip Nation for this new work on the spiritual disciplines. *Habits for Our Holiness* will help you grow deeper in your faith and engage more passionately in God's mission.

—**CHRISTINE CAINE**, author of *Unstoppable: Running the Race You Were Born to Win*

I highly recommend *Habits for Our Holiness*, by my good friend Philip Nation. Like an expert guide, he will take you deep into the heart of God and the spiritual disciplines that Jesus' followers have practiced for two millennia. But then he shows you how your holiness is the fuel that empowers you to join Jesus in his redemptive mission.

—**DERWIN L. GRAY,** lead pastor of Transformation Church, and author of *The High Definition Leader: Building Multiethnic Churches in a Multiethnic World*

HABITS

for Our

HOLINESS

How the Spiritual Disciplines
Grow Us Up, Draw Us Together,
and Send Us Out

Philip Nation

MOODY PUBLISHERS

CHICAGO

Edited by Jim Vincent
Interior design: Ragont Design
Cover design: Simplicated Studio
Author photo: Sheila Martinez Photography

Library of Congress Cataloging-in-Publication Data

Names: Nation, Philip, 1970-
Title: Habits for our holiness : how the spiritual disciplines grow us up,
  draw us together, and send us out / by Philip Nation.
Description: Chicago : Moody Publishers, 2016. | Includes bibliographical
  references.
Identifiers: LCCN 2015039125 | ISBN 9780802413482
Subjects: LCSH: Spiritual life--Christianity. | Christian life.
Classification: LCC BV4501.3 .N379 2016 | DDC 248.4/6--dc23 LC record available
at http://lccn.loc.gov/2015039125

ISBN: 978-0-8024-1348-2

We hope you enjoy this book from Moody Publishers. Our goal is to provide high-quality, thought-provoking books and products that connect truth to your real needs and challenges. For more information on other books and products written and produced from a biblical perspective, go to www.moodypublishers.com or write to:

Moody Publishers
820 N. LaSalle Boulevard
Chicago, IL 60610

1 3 5 7 9 10 8 6 4 2

Printed in the United States of America

To Angie
Your capacity for love and hope always amaze me.
You have my heart.
Today and always.
I love you.

CONTENTS

Introduction

A NEW LOOK
AT OLD PRACTICES

Once upon a time, there lived a people who desperately wanted to be saved from the Dragon Prince. He was a terrible man who appeared to be large but was truly quite small. A master of deception and hateful in his demeanor, he desired nothing but the destruction of the rightful king and his loving followers. But one thing more he desired, to own the affections of the princess of these people. He wanted to own her heart.

So one day he captured Princess Larissa, brought her to his dark homeland, and forced her to live in his cold fortress. But he could never win her heart.

Then a bright and beautiful day arrived for the princess. The valiant king stormed the fortress of the enemy to rescue her. With a mighty blow from his sword, the king defeated the Dragon Prince after a fierce battle.

As he led Princess Larissa back to their kingdom, the people rejoiced. A great celebration broke forth, and the parties that followed were extravagant and seemingly endless. Freedom had been given to the one who had known nothing but captivity. Princess Larissa felt joy and safety and the love of family in a kingdom whose gates can never again be breached.

It's a quaint story, sounding like something you would read your daughter late at night before she drifts off to sleep. Whether you're a guy or a gal, you want it to end properly. You want the bad guy to get beat, the people to be rescued, the princess to be cared for, and the king to march away in victory. It is the way that fairy tales are supposed to end.

The story is emblematic of how we see Christ the King breaking into this dark world on His gospel rescue mission. As we walk through life, we want the assurance that God is not just a passive observer. We need to know that He is active, concerned, and involved. The desire of our heart runs in two directions. We want to know that God will send a Rescuer. And then, in some quiet way, we dare to believe that He might use us in the work of rescuing others.

Throughout my time as a Christian, I've met people who are seeking to find a path to spiritual truth. I see God at work as He has always been at work: calling people to Himself. One such person is Todd (not his real name). Todd wants to believe something but is unsure what that something will be. Amazingly enough, in one conversation before he was a believer, Todd expressed what I want to be the theme for my own relationship with God. He wanted his spiritual journey to be about God and not about his own needs, desires, and dreams. I was shocked, but in a good way. The Holy Spirit was drawing him to the Father. Todd was being led to desire the King rather than the treasures in the kingdom. How different from the pseudo-spirituality we witness in modern media and bestsellers lists promoting *The Gift* and *Scientology*, and the words of Oprah and Chopra.

We have grown accustomed to unbelievers looking for a spiritual path but for selfish reasons. Yet people like Todd further convince me that God is drawing men, women, and children to a relationship that will spread the fame of God throughout the nations. It is the real-life evidence of the biblical truth that God has put eternity in our hearts (Eccl. 3:11). The work that God is doing is to make for Himself a holy people who are set apart for His good work in this world.

Todd is more illustrative of what God is doing in our day than most are aware. He is a real person, but an example of many people attending our churches today. The Father is persuading the people of our day to come and love Him. As we love God in terms of a covenant relationship, then, He in turn can work in us and through us for the sake of His glory. As our lives are transformed by the gospel, we learn to love God as we are loved by God.

In Psalm 138 King David reveals the right view of life:

I will give You thanks with all my heart; I will sing Your praise before the heavenly beings. I will bow down toward Your holy temple and give thanks to Your name for Your constant love and truth. You have exalted Your name and Your promise above everything else. On the day I called, You answered me; You increased strength within me. . . . Though the Lord is exalted, He takes note of the humble; but He knows the haughty from a distance. If I walk into the thick of danger, You will preserve my life from the anger of my enemies. You will extend Your hand; Your right hand will save me. The Lord will fulfill His purpose for me. Lord, Your love is eternal; do not abandon the work of Your hands. (Psalm 138:1–3, 6–8)

We are all drawn to sing the praises of God for all creation to hear. We declare the greatness of God's constant love and faithfulness. We tell it to heavenly beings, kings of the earth, and even to ourselves. There is a complete assurance that God will answer the lowly and encourage the weak. I like the way The Message paraphrases verse 8: "Finish what you started in me, God. Your love is eternal—don't quit on me now."

TEACHING OTHERS TO LOVE GOD

But what are we doing to participate in God's process of teaching others how to love Him? It is the place where we should take what God does in us and carry it to those around us. The models for discipleship in the church today are numerous. But do they accomplish the task? I would say a resounding "No." Most try a Waffle House approach to discipleship: scattered, smothered, and covered. They throw in all of the ingredients to whip up a sad omelet that tastes like everything but really tastes like nothing.

Many of the current models of discipleship and spiritual formation have earth-bound goals. They focus on building up personal knowledge on doctrinal subjects, practicing a few spiritual exercises, personal purpose, and how to be a happier individual. These paradigms develop few deep relationships and even less missional living.

DISCIPLESHIP: PEOPLE CENTERED OR GOD CENTERED?

So where does it fall short? They are people centered. *"What can I do to be fulfilled? What can I do to help my fellow man? What can I do to add to God's kingdom? What must we do differently?"* The commonality that should be inherent in all spiritual growth is love. We must understand this principle: *Love is the central discipline of the Christian life.* Everything else will flow from that as the centerpiece of spiritual formation. Believers should seek to develop their relationship with God through the church resulting with a habitual holiness. All of our biblical skills, prayers, spiritual disciplines, and relationships are used by God as tools to make us holy, make us unified in Him, and set us on fire for His mission.

A great movement is underway in the church to recapture a refreshing sense of spiritual practices. So what is a spiritual discipline? I define it this way:

A spiritual discipline is a mental and physical act and a habit that expresses our love for God and fosters a greater display of His glory in our lives and a deeper understanding of His character and agenda.

In simpler terms, it is the practice of our relationship and theology.

Some are put off by the very term *discipline*. It conjures up images of mean teachers from elementary school days. But the apostle Paul wrote to Timothy with the following words: "Have nothing to do with godless myths and old wives' tales; rather, train yourself to be godly. For physical training is of some value, but godliness has value for all things, holding promise for both the present life and the life to come" (1 Tim. 4:7–8 NIV).

Training ourselves for godliness is spiritual discipline, and it is not oppressive. It allows us to better understand the true life we have inherited because of Christ's redemption. William Law wrote, "For God has made no promises of mercy to the slothful and negligent. His mercy is only offered to our frail and imperfect, but best endeavours, to practise all manner of righteousness."[1] We need to discipline ourselves because, as the Scriptures teach, the things we plant in our lives are the things that grow in our lives (see Gal. 6:7–8).

REASONS FOR THE DISCIPLINES

Throughout this book we will go on a journey to discover that God gives the spiritual disciplines for several reasons. They are not an end to themselves but tools in His hands to mold us. Spiritual disciplines grow us up in the maturity of our faith. Each discipline can be used by God to form you into the likeness of Christ. Through the spiritual disciplines we are seeking to serve as He served, pray as He prayed, and submit as He submitted.

The disciplines can increase our intimacy with God so that we can work to extend His reign in the lives of those around us. I want you to enjoy a deeper walk with Christ as the spiritual disciplines urge you forward in missional living. These disciplines aid us in expressing our love for God and experiencing the love of God.

OUR FAITH, UNWRAPPED

Beyond the internal working that they accomplish, the disciplines have an impact beyond our own lives: they can make a difference in the lives of others. But that happens only when we focus on advancing God's great spiritual enterprise: the reconciliation of all things to Himself, including us. We know that God wants to make us holy; like Jesus. We also know that He wants to redeem other people. The King of the universe has a deeper desire to redeem people than we can begin to imagine. Amazingly, He invites us into the work. When we love Him deeply, He will form us to mirror His heart; and He has a missionary heart.

It is what we instinctively know is wrong with living in a monastery when there is a world filled with spiritual blindness and injustice. We may retreat for time alone to draw close to God, but keeping the truth behind walls is cruel, bordering on heartless. When the truth lays hold of our souls, we should feel the compulsion to share it. We will discover that times of retreat, Sabbath resting, and even silence are part of the spiritual disciplines. At times, we need purposeful separation from the world to gain spiritual perspective and empowerment from the Lord. But holding Jesus and His truth hostage inside of our devotional lives or in holy huddles of believers removes us from His great mission to the world. Separating ourselves from the culture and its people may seem super-spiritual in the moment but concealing our faith has never been God's call.

Let's not keep our faith under wraps but put the gospel's impact on display for the world to see God's transforming work alive in us. It is why we need this journey toward missional spirituality. Christians should never find themselves so deep in a prayer closet that they are unable to see the rest of the world. Those we love should never suffer because of our bid for spiritual maturity. Quite the opposite. The world should benefit from our spiritual growth.

As you take this journey with me, I pray that you will sense God's call for us to return to Him with love and habitual holiness, leading to lives consumed with His glory and mission.

Chapter 1

TRAVELS THROUGH THE GARDEN:

COMING TO LOVE CHRIST

"In the beginning, God . . ."

A nd thus begins the sweeping and true drama we know as Scripture. Within those opening words of Genesis 1:1 rings the truth that God is there, where all things we know find their beginning. He was there before the earth blinked into existence and He will be there when it is no more. He is present when the earth is without its present form. He creates light prior to the existence of the sun. He sets earthly time into motion before the first timepiece enters the mind of man. He creates birds and fish and mammals of such beauty that no one could fathom. This new world showcases the beauty of God's holiness. And in each moment of creation, God deems it as "good" (see Gen. 1:4, 10, 12, 18, 21, 25).

And then comes man. In the midst of the sixth day, God

makes the choice that we would come into existence. He endows man with His own image. The mystery of God's own character or face or type placed into us is beyond our ability to dream. Then, the authority to rule is handed over to this one man. It is not given to the lion or the gorilla. Not the behemoth nor the leviathan. No living creature is to rule except Adam. He alone is given the rights and privileges normally afforded to sovereignty.

In my mind's eye, I picture what it must have been to be the first of our race. Adam and his helpmate Eve experience a shameless life of love for one another. As companions to one another, theirs is a kind rulership over the creatures of earth. Joy, peace, and laughter are the totality of life together. There is no sin as they walk with God.

Into the garden of Eden God placed man and woman. And that would be enough. That God designed and created such a place of wonder and beauty filled with fascinating creatures and plant life is enough for man to know that his Creator cares for them. The anointing of man and woman as stewards of the earth assures them that the Lord has trusted them. Perfect provision given to Adam and Eve shows that God cares for them.

In addition to all that is given to them, God adds the greatest gift of all—His presence. He comes and grants to them His friendship as He walks with them during the cool of the day (3:8). It is within the realm of possibility that God would be too busy for these fragile creations, man and woman. After all, He has the entirety of heaven, all of the universe, and things beyond comprehension to rule. And yet God's love is so deep that He comes to the man and woman for lazy afternoon strolls.

GOD'S PURSUIT OF US

The story of creation seamlessly moves into the story of God's intimate pursuit of relationship with man, woman, and their descendants. After sin enters the picture by the choice of Adam and Eve, we find ourselves marred from birth by our sin nature and relationally separated from God by our own choices to sin. Yet we find ourselves under the missionary gaze of God. In a move that would seem to be contrary to all we deserve, God comes to find us. Both in the garden of Eden and in our everyday living, God calls to us, "Where are you?" He does not ask because somehow He has lost track of us. Rather, He wants us to realize that we have become a far-from-God people. We need to realize that "Aslan is on the move" (as C. S. Lewis wrote[1]) to rescue us from our sin and ourselves.

And why is this? Why would the Creator look for man and woman while they hid in shame? Why does the Potter even concern Himself with clay that resists proper molding? Why does Christ, the Bridegroom, today seek out such a decadent bride? Why?

Love. Love is the answer. Love is what our God extends to us. It is a love relationship that transcends our shackles of sin and self-dependence. God chooses us out of His pure love. In that love, He displays His glory. His very character is that of love. In the midst of His pure justice, He shows love and mercy. When He chooses Abram, it is a choice of love; not based on worthiness. At the time of Israel's unfaithfulness, His love springs forth as He sends judges and prophets to call the "apple of His eye" back to Him.

LOVE'S ARRIVAL

And then comes the Christ. The gospel of Mark records Jesus' first proclamation in ministry as this call: "The kingdom of God has come near. Repent and believe in the good news!" (1:15). As Jesus arrives on the earth, He comes to bring with Him the kingdom. He heralds the good news. He comes bearing the light. And the greatest part of this gospel message is that He is the King of the kingdom, He is the good news, and He is the light of the world. He has come to extend a love to fallen man. Redemption is drawing near. Life is arriving as if it were the dawn of a new day. Let the nations rejoice and all mankind be glad!

So when salvation arrives at our doorstep, a choice is made. We find the gospel illumined in such manner that its truth cannot be denied. Our hearts burn with conviction from the Spirit, and we surrender to Christ. It is the turning point of eternity for every person who chooses the Son as Savior. Redemption arrives. God the Judge is Christ the Savior, and the Spirit is the Comforter who crosses the great chasm in order to catch away the breath of the new bride.

And it is for the glory of His love that we are to return this love. As we consider the great love of the Father, there is no other response that is worthy of the life-giving King of all things. Our thirst and hunger for meaning, purpose, and destiny must suddenly fall away. The Father has sent the Son to die for the sin of man. Lovingly, He has lavished grace upon those who will believe. And now we must respond.

I gave my response many years ago. Kneeling beside the brown sofa in my childhood home, I listened as my father led me to the throne of the King, to whom I was an enemy yet

He was calling me to salvation. On that Sunday morning in 1977, Dad helped me to see that there was a love beyond my young imagination. As the years have progressed, I have come to know that imagination is not necessary. Instead, this love is rooted in such a deep reality that it can never be changed.

HOW WE RETURN GOD'S LOVE

God's love for me deserves the return gift of my own love. Of course, God's love extended to me deserves much more than any of us can give. And yet He requests our love. Love is to be the theme for our life in Him.

Even at the time of Simon Peter's reinstatement, Jesus speaks to him about a standard of love for his Lord. Jesus does not ask:

Simon, will you fast when I am gone?
Simon, will you pray a lot?
Simon, how will you handle money?
Simon, will you lead the coolest church in town?
Simon, will you fight injustice?

No. Instead Jesus asks, "Simon, son of John, do you love Me more than these?" Not once, but three times (John 21:15–17). For Christ, the focal point is love.

If we were in Peter's shoes, we would probably beg Christ, "What can I do to make this up to You? I will do anything to prove myself. Just tell me how." Perhaps that thought ran through Peter's mind. We often equate allegiance with actions. Christ would have us see love as the first form of relationship.

The entire reason for our relationship with Christ is love. It is not to try harder. That would insult the sufficient work of Christ for our salvation. It is not in seeking to earn His affection. That would negate His grace toward our sinfulness. Rather, Christ seeks us out as He did Peter on the shoreline of failure. And on that shore, He calls for our return to love.

FAKE SPIRITUALITY

I have often heard people use a "fake it till you make it" formula for following God. But you cannot fake love. This "fragile stone"[2] we know as Peter cannot fake it at this point. He has been brought too low. Yet many of us are still trying to fake a relationship of love when our hearts are full of rebellion. A spiritual life is something we desire, but our nature seems to fail in attaining it. So we lean on our family heritage of Christianity, religious practice, including church attendance, or a choice to be "spiritual, not religious." It all sounds so good to the human ear. But it causes a gagging of divinity.

God is not calling you to promise greater allegiance through a disciplined life or living out a fake spirituality. He is asking you to love Him for who He is. We are not to love Him to find some nebulous meaning for life or to obtain personal comfort or physical well-being. God's sole intent is that our lives will reflect His love.

In John 8, Jesus was speaking to the Jews who were claiming to be the rightful descendants of Abraham and therefore God's chosen children. Jesus sought to correct them and to show them the true way. After rebuking them for their plot for His execution, He said to them, "If God were your Father, you would love Me, because I came from God and I am here. For I didn't come on My own, but He sent Me" (v. 42). If they were in true relationship with the Father, they would naturally have a love for the Son.

THE COVENANT OF LOVE

A Bond That Is Unbreakable

Jesus assures us of His love in John 15, "As the Father has loved me, I have also loved you. Remain in my love" (v. 9). He reiterates love as central to our relationship. Just as Christ calls for our love, He assures of His love. Love is the covenant that cannot be broken.

O. Palmer Robertson gives a great definition for a covenant: a "bond in blood sovereignly administered."[3] Think about those three elements: It is (1) *a bond* (2) fixed *in blood* that (3) *is sovereignly administered*. First, as *a bond* this covenant has bound believers to Christ because of His work. It is not our work. As Paul wrote, "For it is by grace you have been saved, through faith—and this is not from yourselves, it is the gift of God—not by works, so that no one can boast" (Eph. 2:8–9 NIV). The covenant of love by which we have been captured is solely the work of Christ. If it were by my works, I could easily walk away or fall away because my work is captured by the temporal world of corrosion. But because it is the work done by the eternal Lord, it is a binding that not even hell itself can break, much less my own sinful choices.

Fixed by Blood

Second, a covenant is fixed *in blood*. The covenant we have with Christ is one sealed with His blood, the very life force of the body. When Adam and Eve sinned, an animal was slain so their naked bodies could be covered. The sacrificial system for God's people in the Old Testament was that blood be spilled for sin to be covered. Hebrews 9:22 states that "without the shedding of blood there is no forgiveness." Our only defense and hope is the blood of Christ. It brings peace and righteousness to hopeless men and women. It washes us clean and sings grace over our lives. It is only by the blood of Christ that we can possibly enter into the holy place with God. It is by His blood that we are his people. As Paul reminds us, "The church of God [is] bought with his own blood" (Acts 20:28b NIV). We are a people connected by the shedding of blood by Jesus.

In 2005, I worked with some friends to plant a church. On our launch Sunday, we began a series of messages through the book of Ephesians—not a very common choice when launching a church in an area that is over 60 percent unchurched. On the first Sunday, we used Ephesians 1:7–14 to teach them of "God's Purpose for You." It was important to us that the first point of the first sermon for this new church would be about the blood of Christ. Verse 7 (NIV) reads, "In him we have redemption through his blood, the forgiveness of sins, in accordance with the riches of God's grace."

The temptation was to choose some innocuous series with every sermon being five steps to successful marriage, parenting, work life, or owning a dog. But the blood of Christ is too important to relegate to some future date. It is only with sacrifice that we can come into a relationship with God.

Administered by a Sovereign God

Third, a covenant *is sovereignly administered*. It is not for the creature to determine how we will relate to the Creator. Americans love to talk about our rights. We debate them, fight for them, and elect leaders who will protect them. But in this relationship, God has all the rights and we lay ourselves at His merciful right hand. Does this sound a bit one-sided to you? It is not. Whereas God could constantly pummel us with our sin, He chooses to administrate the covenant with love as the essence of relationship. But we must never lose sight of who exactly is in charge. The Scripture teaches that we love Him because He first loved us (1 John 4:19). He loves us first, He chooses us, He rescues us, He seals us, and He sustains us. God alone has the right to direct our relationship. In return, He asks for our love.

As the central discipline of the Christian life, love is what propels habitual holiness and the desire to follow God into the world for His redeeming mission. Internal transformation (founded in our love for Christ) manifests itself in external action (Bible reading, fellowship, prayer, serving, giving, etc.). It doesn't work the other way around. Performing the (external) spiritual disciplines without a true (internal) love for Christ looks a lot like the Pharisees in action.

We need to be called back to living out of love for Christ and not a self-serving motivation of becoming a better spiritual person. The greatest discipline is love. All of the other disciplines flow from that love. As we love deeply, our lives will be separated for His holy purposes. The more often we hold up love, the more habitual our holiness will become.

HOW LOVE CAN SPRING FORTH

When I finished reading *Celebration of Discipline* by Richard Foster, I just sat quietly for a while. It was the first time I read a book about spiritual disciplines for someone living in the modern era. Granted, with Foster being a Quaker, I differ with him on a number of theological positions. But his desire to enjoy intimacy with Christ was a refreshing challenge. Then I encountered *The Spirit of the Disciplines* by Dallas Willard and my spiritual life was turned on its head. I did not have to be a Quaker or a monk to practice the disciplines. I could be an evangelical and not keep my head in a book all the time. Next I read Brother Lawrence's little book *The Practice of the Presence of God*. In his desire to commune with God at all times I realized how shallow my life had often become.

On one occasion I met Avery Willis, a man whose life in Christ was consumed with a passionate love that shamed me. An ongoing friendship I enjoy with Henry Blackaby constantly bears out how clearly we can know the will of God if we would only allow our love for Him to rule every facet, moment, and arena of life. Serving with friends in the church consistently rewards me with the chance to see how an intense love for Christ will propel me into a missional life that will seek the reign of God over our community. With love as the central discipline of Christian living, all other practices are welcomed as dear friends rather than toilsome acquaintances.

At the end of the day, we must ask ourselves who we want to become. For my part, I want to be like Christ. If only His character and love could flow into me, then I would truly understand the heart of the Father. But I am just a novice. Thomas

Merton once said, "We do not want to be beginners. But let us be convinced of the fact that we will never be anything else but beginners, all our life."[4] So let us begin again. Come with me to discover how love can spring forth through obeying the commands of Christ. Come with me to leave the desert-dwelling and dance on dark mountain peaks. Come and train your attention on the relationship of love He has for us rather than the multitude of distracting environments of this distressing world. Come back to the garden with me.

Chapter 2

OUR SOUL'S DESIRE AND DESIGN:

THE PRACTICE OF WORSHIP

Worship is the central activity of every person's existence. If for some reason you don't believe that, then take a look around at your own life. A quick peek at your calendar and bank accounts will reveal that we worship something. In its most crude form, worship is obsessing over something. We find it in how we treat our relationships and in the modern practice of binge-watching television shows. Though we often think of worship as singing songs in a service, it is much more. Worship is giving your affections away to someone or something.

We were created to relate to God in an intimate fashion. By coming so close to Him, we cannot but worship. Surely He is the one worthy of receiving our affections. Why? His character is righteous. His presence is beautiful. His work is perfect. Worship is the only logical response to Him. It is our response to God's initiating work in our lives. William Temple wrote, "To worship is to quicken the conscience by the holiness of God, to feed the mind with the truth of God, to purge the imagination by the beauty of God, to open the heart to the love of God, to devote the will to the purpose of God."[1] Such worship can easily be summed up by loving Him supremely.

The great commandment of God is to love the Lord with our whole being (Matt. 22:37–38). The expression of that love is worship. Love must not allow itself to degenerate to mere behavior modification in the hopes of pleasing a distant deity. Instead, worship is the intimate encounter that mortals have with our immortal God. Dallas Willard wrote, "In worship we engage ourselves with, dwell upon, and express the greatness, beauty, and goodness of God through thought and the use of words, rituals, and symbols."[2] At its heart, worship is to ascribe worth. As we worship the Lord, we are declaring to Him and to all of creation that He is the most worthy to receive honor and adoration.

Psalm 95 reminds us that worship is necessary and joyful. It is based on the way that God graciously works. When we see how deeply He loves us then it is easy to worship. Here are the first seven verses of that psalm:

> Come, let us shout joyfully to the Lord, shout triumphantly to the rock of our salvation! Let us enter His presence with thanksgiving; let us shout triumphantly to Him in song. For the Lord is a great God, a great King above all gods. The depths of the earth are in His hand, and the mountain peaks are His. The sea is His; He made it. His hands formed the dry land. Come, let us worship and bow down; let us kneel before the Lord our Maker. For He is our God, and we are the people of His pasture, the sheep under His care.

To the world, worship is just what occurs when people gather in a holy place to talk about holy things. Yes, worship happens when God's people gather but it must extend beyond that. Worship should occur both in our gathering and in our living when we are not gathered. All of what is to follow will be a wandering back and forth between your private devotional life and how we live as the community of faith. Instead, the word "worship" has come to mean something that occurs only in a church's building on Sundays when everyone is gathered for an hour. We should see it as that and more.

UNFOCUSED LOVE

Every person will worship something or someone. For you and me as believers, it must become habitual to worship only God. But in reality we often break the great command by God to love Him with all our heart, soul, mind, and strength (Mark 12:30). God wants us to worship Him with our complete self, but we often give Him only a fraction of who we are. Consider the people, issues, and circumstances of life that currently cry out for you to worship them. These people and issues do not ask you to sing songs to them, but they do demand your total allegiance. When you surrender just a portion—even only 1 percent—to anyone, it is idolatry. No statues or pagan temples are required for idolatry to take hold of your heart, only that something or someone takes hold of your heart.

Worship as a spiritual discipline focuses our heart's affections fully on our Lord. It is a declaration from our heart, lips, and actions. It is also a rejection as well: when we worship God, we say to everything else, "You are not God." At the same time, worship is an act of holiness. It sets our heart's affections and mind's attention apart for God, His covenant of grace, and His mission to the world. Then, in beautiful form, we can practice it in private and in public.

PRIVATE WORSHIP

Worship is an intensely personal activity. In it, we lay our souls before the everlasting God with the intent of His dominion over us. To do that well, it must often be done in the secret realms of our soul. Yet it is not secret in the sense that no one else knows about it, for its outward results include joy, peace, and declarations of God's goodness.

Worship transpires when we show the willingness for God to penetrate every arena of our life; thoughts, desires, hopes, ambitions, relationships, possessions—everything. It is happening when we likewise seek to place our mind's attention and heart's affection solely on God. Every thought is taken captive for Him. Each possession and relationship placed under His sovereign rule. All of our vain ambitions cast aside as we hold on deeply to His greatness and His great adventure of how we might live. To worship God in such a way should color our private, daily devotions.

Through Daily Devotions

The intent of a daily devotional time is to gather regularly and intimately with God. Unfortunately, for some Christians this has become a legalistic checkbox on the day. In fact, our own desires and our enemy Satan want it to become a transactional thought in our minds. If I show up, then God owes me something. But that has never been God's intention. He is not interested in swapping favors with you. God wants your heart. For that to occur, we need to focus on God's message to us.

Whether you set aside a time in the morning or evening, your daily devotion must center upon God's Word. The Bible is how God has chosen to reveal Himself to us, so we must listen to it closely. Wrap your life around the Scriptures so that you will not be drawn away by myths or the pseudo-wisdom of the world. In the next chapter, I will discuss the role of the Bible and methods to study it. So for the purpose here of worship, allow me to deal more with our priorities of how we worship through it.

Recite Scripture to the Lord. In your own devotions, at times you may be at a loss for words. The loss comes from every end of the spectrum. When you have committed the same sin so many times, you just don't know what to say to God. It is time to simply immerse yourself in the Scriptures that speak of His unending desire to reconcile you. When the pain of life is too great to verbalize, the Word is filled with God's people crying to Him at their point of loss. As we experience victories and joy in life, our own vocabulary is sometimes insufficient. Turning to the Word and repeating it to God is the solution in all of these.

Honesty before God comes more naturally when we read of disciples, prophets, and even kings who blew it but came humbly to our God who readily forgives. Faith is more easily exercised as you visit the stories of God's provisions for the widow, orphan, and outcast. Courage for sharing our faith increases as we rehearse the stories of the early church in Acts and Paul's missionary journeys throughout his letters. Holiness becomes more realistic in our culture when we read God's call to the faithful who lived in the anti-God cultures of Babylon and the Roman Empire.

In our personal time of reading, there are applications awaiting, especially when we pray for direction and insight through the Holy Spirit before we begin our reading and study.

Through Prayer

Prayer is an intensely intimate act. Later in this book, we will take a look at how prayer works and the role of fasting in our lives. But for now, consider prayer as an act of worship. When we pray, we enter into a new posture. Prayer requires worship, at least if it is done with the right attitude. In prayer, you recognize that there is One greater than you and you are needful of His intervention in your life. In prayer, you are pleased to bow in loving submission and listen with attentiveness.

Through Singing . . . Alone

We sing in the light of life's joys. We sing in the dark of its valleys. Singing is a natural form of expression in the human experience. No matter what corner of the planet you visit, whether a megacity or a mountaintop village, you'll find people whistling, humming, and singing to express their emotions. In our private life of worship, singing is a powerful expression. These songs are at times spontaneous, and there are times for singing alone.

When we sing, it is often due to the joy soaring in our hearts. Worship by song is often an emotional expression, especially songs of joy and faith. In fact, the song of your heart can often be an indication of your level of faith in the gospel's hope. The lack of celebration in our personal worship should certainly alert us toward a waning level of faith. But when we tap into the lyrics of a great song with a beautiful melody, it allows us a moment of passionate declaration to God that we know He is true and He is trustworthy.

Through Weeping

Life is hard. In our lives, we experience death, sickness, unemployment, rejection, and all manner of oppression from the world. In worship, we are able to weep before God as the cry of the needy toward the One who can provide. When we lament before God, it is an act of worship like none other. We cry to Him as the only One who can make any difference in our circumstances. When we cry in our private worship, it is done to abandon our life's needs to God.

Jesus Himself wept before the Father. Just before His arrest in the garden of Gethsemane, the Messiah grieved so intensely His sweat became thick "like drops of blood" (Luke 22:44; cf. Matt. 26:37). It is not a shameful thing to shed tears while before the Lord. It is the acknowledgment of our own helplessness before our omnipotent God.

Others in the Bible followed a similar path. One of my favorite people to follow in this is the prophet Jeremiah, who has been called the weeping prophet. After all, the companion book of his in the Old Testament is titled Lamentations. With Jeremiah, we see a man who was stalwart when before the people. In delivering the prophecies given to him by the Lord, he did so with a strong voice and a courageous life. But his private life revealed a broken and sometimes distraught man. As Jeremiah spent time with the Lord, he would cry out in tears. Perhaps those tears are what created a difference for him. Jeremiah's weeping before God strengthened him before the people.

PUBLIC WORSHIP

Daily private worship benefits our relationship with God and our growth in the faith. But public worship with the community of faith has the same impact. The loss of either one puts us on shaky ground. Private worship and public worship feed one another. We can be tempted to privatize our worship, but doing so can keep us from God's power at work in the Christian community. Our faith is best lived out when we do so together.

Public worship reminds us of Christ's promises to the church. Our public worship is done as a declaration to God that He is great and His Son is King. Such joyful worship also declares to the world the greatness of the Father and the Son.

Why We Worship Together

The Bible contains both the description of how people worship God and prescriptive teachings about how we are to worship the Lord. Worship is one of the primary functions in the life of the church family. It is a spiritual discipline that feels natural when done in community. The challenge is for us to retain it as a spiritual discipline and not a religious activity that attempts to win favor with God.

We are easily given over to legalism. Worship often rises to the top of our religious activity checklist. We may not say it, but we can easily think it: *I went to worship this week, so God should look out for me this week. I'll check in again next Sunday to show my devotion.* Such an attitude completely misses the point of worshiping together. In fact, it is the opposite of worship. In corporate worship, we are collectively saying that God is worthy of our attention and are reminded that such gathered worship honors God. We cannot think that our attendance somehow obligates God to certain advocacy on behalf of ourselves or the local church. We worship to show the centrality of God in all things, to assert His goodness, and to remind us of the joy of serving Him.

Singing Together

Christians are a singing people. Throughout the Scriptures, we witness the melodies of God's people in worship. The entire book of Psalms is the ancient hymnbook of the Israelites. Within its pages are songs that celebrate God's goodness and call for His judgment upon sinners. We must not give in to any low-level, Prom-songs-to-Jesus mentality that simply places Him on the level of a pop-rock boy band. We have been given access to the King of the universe, not our favorite member of a music group. He is the God of the universe who has called us "friend." We should not dare to treat our relationship with Him lightly. We sing because God the Son has made Himself known. We sing because we have experienced eternal grace in our salvation. We sing because we desire to honor His holy name.

Paul taught that the church is to speak "to one another in psalms, hymns, and spiritual songs, singing and making music from your heart to the Lord" (Eph. 5:19). When the community of faith worships together, it can and should include the variety of music called for by Paul. So before we get too bogged down in the style, ensure that your church worships as we are called to do so: "from your heart."

Now, some of what we've traditionally called singing in the Bible is actually recitations of truths. For example, in the Gospels, the angels did not sing at the Messiah's birth. Instead, they called out to one another. The same is true in many other places. So, perhaps, when we think about the church singing, we can also consider the category a bit more broadly in how we declare things together. When a congregation recites a doctrinal creed together or participates in a responsive reading, we are effectively singing the song of our faith (even though a melody may not be present).

Worshiping with our voices united must be treated as a spiritual endeavor. As the church unites our voices, it creates a powerful testimony of our faith to God. It draws us together in the sacrifice of praise. We find strength in our unity and seek for God's blessing on our corporate ministry.

Praying in Community

Though I'll discuss prayer at length in two other chapters and the prayer of adoration in this chapter, I do not want you to miss the worshipful nature of prayer. In our prayers, we submit to and praise God as a community of faith. *Our* prayers take on different forms at times than *my* prayers.

Prayer is an act of worship by the community of believers. In it, we are agreeing to take a submissive position before the matchless King. When we pray alone, we cry out for ourselves and others. In praying together, we are following the biblical teaching to put our hearts in unity and agree on what God desires to accomplish. Prayer, as a church, is not just something for our religious checkmark. It is a way that we relationally engage with God about His heart and His will.

Consider all the ways that you can pray together with the community of faith. We pray in Bible study groups and in the worship service. It happens for the offering, over the Lord's Supper, and during ordination services. We pray with and for one another when there is suffering. Praying together brings our wills into agreement with God's sovereign plan. Relationally, it expresses our love for Him as a person and as His people. Each time we pray together we are following Jesus' teaching.

Many in secular society will rail against and work against such worship-filled declarations from our lips or our lives. We will be told, "Prayer is useless. No one is listening. It's just wishful thinking to hope that some anonymous deity in the heavens will listen to you." But Jesus revealed something altogether different. He told His disciples: "Again, I assure you: If two of you on earth agree about any matter that you pray for, it will be done for you by My Father in heaven. For where two or three are gathered together in My name, I am there among them" (Matt. 18:19–20).

God gives us a promise. When we will unify our hearts under His powerful grace, He answers. Prayer is a moment of worship when God's people declare that He is true and trustworthy.

Public prayer should include adoration. Together we esteem the character of God. It is different from the act of thanksgiving. Adoration

Adoration is loving God for who He is, whereas thanksgiving is praising Him for His activity. Both are necessary.

is loving God for who He is, whereas thanksgiving is praising Him for His activity. Both are necessary, but let's focus on how the whole church can worship God in the prayer of adoration.

In his book simply titled *Prayer*, Peter Kreeft described adoration as "Absolute respect. Acknowledging that God is God: unique, perfect, absolute, infinite, totally worthy of all our praise and all our love."[3] Such a declaration helps us to remember that worship—both privately and in the community of faith—is a response to the overtures of love from God. Worship is our reciprocal response to God's faithfulness. It is a way that we collectively give respect to God.

When Jesus spoke to the anonymous Samaritan woman at the well in John 4, He described the kind of worship that is required of us. As a Samaritan, she was vaguely familiar with the practices of the Jewish people but happy to remain settled in her own traditions. Jesus told her, "You Samaritans worship what you do not know. We worship what we do know, because salvation is from the Jews. But an hour is coming, and is now here, when the true worshipers will worship the Father in spirit and truth. Yes, the Father wants such people to worship Him. God is spirit, and those who worship Him must worship in spirit and truth" (John 4:22–24). Jesus pointed out that the worship of the Samaritans was—in a word—ignorant. Not in the derogatory sense. Rather, they simply were unaware and had no knowledge of who they were attempting to worship. The Jews, on the other hand, were engaged in an intelligent worship. They knew the one true God and understood that He was planning on sending the Messiah.

Then, we receive the best part about how to worship because Jesus offered her entrance into the inclusive worship that is for all people. It is the beauty of the gospel that reveals our entryway to truly adoring God. The gospel fundamentally changes who we are so that we can move from an existence of constant rebellion to one of pure worship.

TRUE WORSHIP: SPIRIT *AND* TRUTH

Jesus described our worship as twofold. We are to worship, first, in spirit. By worshiping in spirit, we are living in harmony with God. We hide nothing from Him. Additionally, by worshiping in spirit, we are not bound to any one location. As individuals or in community, we can engage in the activities of worship wherever we are. It is a beautiful liberty to know this truth. When the church gathers on Sundays in a sanctuary, we can worship. Or when we sit at a dinner table at a local restaurant, even there, a worship service can break forth if we allow it, with spiritual and God-centered conversations with the people we are eating with.

We also worship God in truth. The dual impact is that we do it with sincerity of our character and in accordance with God's Word. Worship is not just about saying nice things about God. It is a heartfelt declaration of the truth about God. We can only do this once we've encountered the Messiah's salvation and allowed His Word to guide our worship. In the company of believers, this occurs when we allow the gospel to not just move us over the threshold of faith but completely guide our every activity together.

The prayers of adoration that we engage in as a gathered people often focus on the largest of all issues. However, as C. S.

Lewis wrote, we should show God "adoration in the infinitesi-mals" of life as well.[4] We should dwell on the largest of theological ideas such as God's holiness, mercy, beauty, and omnipotence. But we shouldn't neglect giving thanks for the smallest of provisions from Him.

The cry of Psalm 63:1 is "God, You are *my* God" (emphasis added). Adoration is a personal activity but it should not be an exclusively private activity. It is likely that you can apply that statement to each of the spiritual disciplines. Our faith is intensely personal but is to be shared with the faithful and unbelieving alike.

Declaring God's Word

In our public worship in churches or in gatherings with any size group of believers, the Word must play a central role. As the authoritative revelation by God to us, if we leave it out, most of what we do will simply be aimless thinking. But because we have His Word, we can think and say and declare what is right about God.

In our communal worship, the Word plays numerous roles. For many, its most prominent place is when a pastor preaches on a biblical passage to expose to the rest of us the truth of the Bible. As the pastor teaches, it is to give the sense of the passage regarding its impact on eternity and its application for daily living. The Bible consistently points us, toward the good news that the Jesus is the Son of God, once crucified and now risen from the dead.

The preaching of God's Word should not be a time to simply sit down and soak in, but to actively celebrate. In some congregations, this takes the form of responding to the pastor during the message with the "amens" of agreement. In other worship gatherings, it is with quieter joys in the heart. No matter how we celebrate the Word, we must. It is eternal and will never pass away.

Declaring God's Word in community extends beyond a pastor's message. There are several other ways the Bible can assist during our public worship:

- Public reading of the Scriptures.
- Singing the songs within the Psalms and other places in the Bible.
- Reciting the Word together.
- Memorizing the Scriptures together.
- Reading through the same passages.

Some might think that this is just the normal order of elements for a worship service. But it must not become mere repetition. All of this is a discipline of our love for God that is lived out together in the fellowship of faith. As we encounter the Word together, it is an intellectual journey but not only an intellectual journey. When we interact with the Word, we are coming to know the God who authored it. It is a moment for elation and worship together as God's people.

All of what has been described is generally attributed to the largest gatherings of our congregations. But worship will often be manifest in smaller gatherings of God's people as well: in Bible studies, small groups, home groups, and accountability groups.

Small groups of every sort gather for a specific purpose the leaders of the church have deemed helpful. No matter what the cause, however, the call should primarily be to gather our lives around the Word in order to worship the King. Keep in mind that worship is not always about singing. In fact, for some, singing in a small group would be so awkward that worship would likely never happen. However, to share the story of God's grace in action in someone's workplace—that's worship.

Testifying of God's Goodness

Because our worship is something to be shared, it should—it must—include the real stories of our lives. In a day of perfectly timed worship services, too many of us church leaders have voluntarily given up on a great blessing. We opt for the security of an overly planned service order rather than the raw, emotional, unrehearsed testimony from God's people. Now, I'm not advocating that ministry leaders never plan out a worship service in favor of "let's just see what happens when we get together" mentality. However, church leaders and congregants alike benefit from listening to the stories from other believers while in worship and in small groups. The power of a person's testimony is in learning to see God's power at work in the world today.

This is why baptism is so powerful. Beyond the act being a symbol of a person's death, burial, and resurrection in Christ, their testimony of salvation is a powerful testimony of worship. Through it, we also cross a bridge between worship and mission. Baptism, along with many other acts of communal worship, becomes a declaration of the gospel to those who are dying in their sins.

The same can be said of receiving the Lord's Supper. In 1 Corinthians 11, Paul taught that when we take Communion, we "proclaim the Lord's death until He comes" (v. 26). The celebration of Christ's body and blood is a look back to what He did. It is a look inside as we examine ourselves to ensure we are worthy to participate in this act of worship. It is also a look ahead that He will one day return.

The worship we do together when a believer tells their story of God's work, a convert is baptized, or the church partakes of the Lord's Supper is all a testimony of God's grace. We do so to declare God's great worth.

THE RESULT OF WORSHIP: MISSION

When we worship, it is not just an insider's exercise for the church. We worship because of both our beliefs and our mission. Worship is an opportunity for an unbelieving world to look over our shoulders and see the celebration of the gospel. Here are a few guiding principles to help us in this community worship.

First, the worship of the church should spill into everyday language. If God is the most important Person in the universe— and He is—then we should speak about Him. I'm married and have two sons. I talk about my family a great deal. Why? Because I love them and they love me. We share our lives together. You likely do the same about your family or closest friends. And yet, there is an odd hesitation in many of our lives when it comes to talking about God.

We should speak often about the beauty of the cross and the greatness of our God. Since God is worthy of our praise, we should give it to Him in the everyday language of our lives. It allows unbelievers to hear about the hope they secretly long to possess.

An unashamed vocabulary about the role of God should exist in our lives. Worshiping regularly in the pace of normal occurrences can drive us toward mission because people are missing out on the glories of Christ. Then, disciple-making becomes the natural outcome of everything we do. Worship will produce disciples.

Second, we should worship in a way that puts people in awe of God. I put this here as much as a warning as I do a principle. No matter the style of a church's worship service, we rightly want to do it with excellence. But excellence can become the point rather than the vehicle. When we worship, there must be an aim. Our goal is for people to leave the church saying, "Those people serve a great God." We should worship in such a way through daily living and corporate gatherings that the lost will be in awe of the greatness of our God.

Third, worship at church should teach our children to worship. Our worship is setting the stage for the next generation of worshipers. Whether you are a parent or not, how you worship with your church (and in your life) is giving an example to children around you. If you worship with an anemic spirit, then they will simply skip it altogether seeing that it is not important. So, we should have a passionate heart toward praise. The children around us should witness adults who have praise constantly on our lips.

Fourth, small groups should worship together. Your Bible study group might be known as a home group, Sunday school class, or any number of other names. Whatever you call it, those who are new to the group should witness its members in worship. The group should not gather for one person to give a lecture like a college class. Nor should the group meet simply to socialize with food. Instead, as we welcome unbelievers into our small group, they should see worship existing inside of our closest relationships.

For the unbeliever, it will likely be unexpected. They will assume the gathering is a place of intellectual give-and-take. Perhaps they have an idea that the group cares for its members. Again, those are healthy parts of a small group. But what the unbeliever needs to witness is a group of people who have joyfully abandoned their lives to a covenant with God.

THROUGH ALL ETERNITY

As Brother Lawrence wrote in *The Practice of the Presence of God,* "The end we ought to propose to ourselves is to become, in this life, the most perfect worshippers of God we can possible be, as we hope to be through all eternity."[5] Worship is a discipline of love, not duty. When done with regularity, it separates our hearts from all the world's demands for its allegiances. A regular practice of worship expresses our love to God and shows it to the world.

Chapter 3

FROM THE HEAD TO THE HEART:

THE PRACTICE OF BIBLE STUDY

The first thing that came to my mind when I was in college and heard the word "study" was something along the lines of a groan. I was bad at it, didn't enjoy it, and generally was easily distracted from it.

By nature, I'm a bit of an information junkie but it is usually about an unrelated mass of information. It's eclectic. Knowing about politics, superhero movies, college football, and other random pop-culture information is fun. Studying is not.

It's that way for many people. And that's why many Christians suffer from immaturity their whole lives. Having come to know Jesus, they never really study to grow in their faith. The Scripture that could grow them up, draw them close to the church, and propel them out to God's mission simply sits as an idle companion to their boring religious life. They have decided that Bible study is too tedious. By ignoring it, they ignore their own growth.

We've all had seasons like it. But when we do, temptation more easily turns to sinful action. Cynicism about other believers creeps in because our discernment is gone. Passiveness about God's mission becomes our natural posture. When we do not allow God to speak His powerful truth through His Word, spiritual apathy and sin become the habit.

But I've learned to embrace the discipline of study. By studying the Bible, it has drawn me not only closer to God but closer to the church and the work we have in front of us. By digging into other great Christian writing, it has helped me better understand how God is working in us to accomplish His purposes. Regularly engaging the Word produces a habitual holiness fueled by God's truth and grace.

WHY THE BIBLE?

The Bible is unlike any other book. It stands at the center point of our faith to tell us who God is. In fact, theologians refer to the Bible as the "special revelation" of divinity. When we look around at nature, the universe, and all of creation, we witness a general revelation. The very existence of order to the universe, the fine-tuning of our bodies to operate, shared joy in relationships, and the beauty of what we experience all represent a *general* revelation that God is present.

The Bible is a special revelation not only to the existence of God but that He wants to reveal Himself to us. God has no interest in remaining distant or relationally removed from us. Instead, He has actively spoken to us with authority through the

Scriptures. We find that the totality of the Scripture is useful. Second Timothy 3:16–17 teaches us:

> All Scripture is inspired by God and is profitable for teaching, for rebuking, for correcting, for training in righteousness, so that the man of God may be complete, equipped for every good work.

The apostle Paul was writing to Timothy about how to lead a church. In doing so, he reveals why the Bible is so vital to our spiritual lives. The leather-bound book sitting on your shelf or the electronic version residing on your smartphone/tablet/ Internet browser window is unlike any other book we could dream up. As Paul describes the Scriptures:

- *They are inspired by God.* God has literally "breathed out" the Scriptures into the minds and hearts of the authors who wrote them down. It comes from the heart and mind of God.
- *They are profitable.* We are not dealing with a book that helps on a few occasions. It benefits your life each time you pick it up.
- *They teach, rebuke, correct, and train.* The Scriptures address the entire life of a person. They impart knowledge that can be trusted, correction that is always needed, and preparation for every assignment. Since God calls us, He intends to equip us.

The Bible consists of sixty-six books written by more than forty writers across three continents and spanning more than

1,500 years—yet it is one story. It is the story of God telling us who He is and how we can be reconciled to Him. Pretty amazing.

HOW TO STUDY THE BIBLE

Recognize Its Themes

Once you've decided (and you probably have) that growing in your faith means studying the Bible, let me give you a few guidelines to help you along the process. First, seek to understand the major themes that guide how we will interact with it.

I think there are three major themes to consider: kingdom, covenant, and mission. The Bible teaches that God has a *kingdom* that will never fail. It cannot be overthrown. The kingdom is God's rightful rule over all things because He is the Creator of all things and by Him all things continue to exist. The church (the local gatherings of believers and the worldwide, history-spanning group of believers) is a part of God's kingdom. As the church, we are a sign of the kingdom and persuade people to serve the King.

Second, the theme of *covenant* pervades the Bible. In God's economy, He wants you to enter His kingdom through His covenant, offered on the terms of the King, which we must accept. This covenant is actually an agreement made in blood and sealed by commitments. Jesus' blood is His commitment of love and righteousness to believers. Repentance and faith is our commitment to His rulership. The covenant of God never fails because He, the faithful one, is at its foundation.

Third, the *mission* of God is seen throughout the Bible. God set Adam and Eve in the garden of Eden with the intention of lovingly ruling their lives in a relationship that allowed them to fulfill His plans. When they sinned, it was God who chased after them. Fast-forward through history to us and we get the same treatment. God pursues us and then invites us to join Him in the ministry of reconciliation toward everyone else (2 Cor. 5).

> *Jesus' blood is His commitment of love and righteousness to believers.*

With those three themes in the background, let's take a look at a simple formula for studying the Bible. It starts with context, then continues with the right questions and being willing to study comprehensively—both in private and with others. It ends with acting upon the truth.

Know the Context

A basic principle of studying Scripture is that you must know the context of a passage to understand the impact of it. If you pluck a verse out of context, well, that's how we get heresy. A verse fits in the context of the passage that fits in the context of the book that fits in the context of the Bible that fits in the context of God's kingdom. It will require that you do some study outside of your Bible passage but it is completely worth it. Take some time to look at a study Bible or a one-volume commentary to get a sense as to what the whole book is about and how the passage fits into the book.

Ask the Right Questions

The next step is to ask the right questions. A strong set of questions will do two things for you. It will keep you from simply looking for how the passage makes you feel. Certainly, our emotions are a valid part of our existence, but our emotions should not be the masters of the interpretation process concerning the Word. Also, it will give you an objective trajectory toward understanding the Bible. Questions built on a good interpretive process will guide you to truth and keep you out of the "what it means to me" subjective mode.

Whether I'm studying for something personal or for a sermon to preach before others, I ask six basic questions. Let me give you each one with some explanation.

1. How Does This Verse or Passage Reveal God's Character?

The Bible is first and foremost about God. He is the main character of every story. In Genesis, it is not about Moses or Abraham. Throughout Israel's history, it is not about King David or his son Solomon. It is not the prophets or the apostles. Every passage we look into tells us something about the nature of God. The Bible is God's personal revelation about who He is.

If God only wanted us to know the facts about a removed deity, then there would be no need for the stories, the poetry, and the constant reminders of His presence among us. As you study, search for the ways in which God is not just revealing theological factoids but personally telling about who He is in relation to you. *The Bible is the epic story of how God wants to reconcile all things to Himself.*

This overarching narrative leads us to the second question.

2. How Does the Passage Reveal God's Redemptive Plan?

With our major themes of kingdom, covenant, and mission, looking for the redemptive work of God in a passage is a natural step. Not every passage will deal pointedly with this idea. But every theological concept, call for repentance, and teaching of how to live out our faith fits into how God is working to reconcile people to Himself.

As you work through a passage, it will fit into the larger narrative of how God is redeeming all things. But you must look for it. Our default position in understanding the Bible is often self-centered. We often look first at how the passage will help us in our daily lives. Certainly, all of the Scriptures will help you and me to live better. But let's prioritize a bit. Our daily lives fit into God's greater plans. By understanding how the passage speaks to His bigger plan, it helps us to fit our life into it and not the other way around.

3. How Did the Passage Apply to the Original Hearers?

I had a professor in seminary who would always say, "There are three keys to understanding any passage: context, context, context." One layer of context you need to discover is what the passage meant when it was first declared. It would be incoherent for a passage to mean something substantially different now than when it was first heard. God is not looking to fool us or make it difficult to understand who He is or how He works. Therefore the meaning of His Word will hold consistently across the ages.

We must, however, work at understanding the nuances of cultural references and things like literary genre as we study the Word. For example, when Paul told the believers in Thessalonica to "greet all the brothers with a holy kiss" (1 Thess. 5:26), what was he telling them to do? What is he telling us to do? The context helps us to understand that there is not necessarily a command to kiss. Rather, it directs us to joyfully greet one another, however that might look in a particular culture. It is more about hospitality and relationships than it is about whether we shake hands, hug, kiss, or fist bump.

4. How Does This Truth Affect My Relationship with Christ?

At this point, we need to pivot from the objective truths to the personal implications. With every Bible passage revealing something about God and how He is reconciling things to Himself, we need to ask how it personally affects us. The Bible's grand story is that God is glorified through our redemption. As you are mining for the truth in the passage, remember the objective is to see how it personally applies in your relationship to Christ. Asking how it informs, changes, or challenges your level of intimacy with God is an important step to take.

The temptation we consistently face in handling the Bible is to treat it as something that will simply modify our behavior. But the gospel is first about transforming your heart by Christ's power and the presence of the Holy Spirit (John 14:15–17, 26; Gal. 5:22–25). Then, through the Spirit's power, your life will be affected. As you search through a passage, look for the ways that it addresses how you relate to Jesus. Then, from that understanding, we can better live out of the power given to us by the Holy Spirit.

5. In What Ways Do I Rebel against the Truth in the Passage?

Let's own up to the fact that we are, by nature, rebels and rogues. Once we have been saved by God's grace, He then spends the rest of our lives making us more like Jesus. But, in the meantime, we still give in to sinful thinking and living.

As you study the Scriptures, you must identify your natural

rebellious tendencies before you step out into the "real world." A new question that you may not be accustomed to asking is about your own mental objections to the truth in a passage. Whether you are a new believer or have been following Jesus for a long time, you—and I—need to own up to the idea that we believe things that are wrong. The Holy Spirit will use the truth of the Bible to change our thinking. We also need to face how we will rebel in our actions against the truth we encounter.

We likely have habitual sins and common tendencies that run counter to God's righteousness. We must be willing to surrender our minds and actions to Him so we can gain a clearer understanding of His revelation. But let's take it one more step. While you study, look into your own life and search yourself for the natural tendencies you have toward rebellion. Once you've identified those fleshly temptations, you can study with greater insight. You can also become involved with other members of the church to hold you accountable.

6. What Is the Impact of the Passage on the Church?

The study of the Bible is an intensely personal discipline. But that does not mean that it must be an exclusively private discipline. As we study, we should look for the applications that the passage has on the life of the entire church. As members of the church—known as the body of Christ (Eph. 1:22–23; Col. 1:18, 24)—what happens in our individual lives will affect what happens in the lives of others and vice versa. It is easier to do this when we hear a pastor preach in worship services or someone else teach during a Bible study. Take that impulse and apply to every encounter you have with the Bible in private. It is going to inform us about how we relate to one another as believers and how we are to move forward together on God's mission.

These six questions are just starting points. As you investigate passages of the Bible, you'll learn to move past the questions in their general forms and ask even more specific questions about issues ranging from God's self-revelation to our life with other believers.

All approaches to the study of the Scriptures still require the ministry of the Holy Spirit in the believer to be effective. Jesus promised the Spirit's presence and that He would be our Teacher (John 14:16–17, 26). Bible study also requires that we recognize the authority and reliability of the Scriptures. With that in mind, here are three cautionary reminders as you study the Bible:

1. Only God can reveal spiritual truths to us. We cannot understand God's Word by studying it on our own apart from Him (Eph. 1:17; 1 Cor. 2:10–13).
2. The Bible shouldn't be studied like it's a history textbook; it is the living and active Word of God (Heb. 4:12).
3. Treating the Bible merely as a guide to moral living will only end in frustration. Developing a moral standard for ourselves and others has never been God's intention. Rather, the truths of the Bible are to be first transformational to the eternal state of our souls and consequently sanctifying to our daily living.

Study Particularly and Comprehensively

Study Alone

The Bible offers much if we are willing, as good students, to spend time in it. Keep in mind our current Bible looks very differently now than when recorded centuries ago by its original human authors. Originally written on scrolls, those original manuscripts did not have chapter and verse numbers. Today's Bible translations offer not only chapter and verse divisions, but many include footnotes, annotations, study notes, maps, and the like. Among the more popular Bible translations with helps are the English Standard Version, the Holman Christian Standard Bible, the New American Standard Bible, the New King James version, and the New International Version.

To best study the Bible, you must become spiritually ambidextrous. In other words, you have to be able to move in two directions: you must study the Scriptures particularly and comprehensively.

You need to study the Bible very *particularly*. Of course, chapter and verse numbers gives you a natural place to start and stop. It helps you to center in on a single verse, one paragraph, or a certain story. We need to study the Bible that specifically. As we believe that God has inspired the Bible, it means every word, verb tense, and nuance of each phrase was divinely ordered. Doing word studies, thinking through the details of every recorded story, and picking apart every phrase offers great benefits. Each detail has meaning. In fact, you can spend a lifetime working through it all and never feel as if you're done. And that is a good thing. Every detail of the Scriptures is meaningful. Studying it will drive us to understand the beauty of God's revelation and its application into our lives.

The other direction to take is to read it *comprehensively*. As a teenager, I began the practice of having a daily quiet time. I was encouraged to read a chapter a day and did so—even when I did not finish a particular story. Though I was reading regularly, I was missing out on the point of many of the stories. The Bible was initially delivered and consumed in large portions. For example, think about the letter that Paul wrote to the church at Ephesus. We call it Ephesians and it has been divided into six chapters. No one believes that the leaders of the Ephesian church read one-sixth of the book and then stopped. I really doubt they said, "Okay, everyone, we'll pick up in this spot tomorrow." It is much more likely that they read it aloud in its entirety.

Nehemiah 8 in the Old Testament reports that the people of God had forgotten the Law of the Lord for a very long time. The people realized it and begged for God's Word to be read to them. Everyone stood in the city square while Ezra the priest read the Law from daybreak until noon (v. 3). For roughly six hours, people stood while the Scriptures were read to them. Longer than a blockbuster movie. Longer than a Super Bowl. Longer than a concert. Longer than most any other activity that we do.

Why? Because they wanted to hear the whole thing. You and I need to fight the temptation of being bored by the Word. It is a shame that we have to fight such a devious temptation, but we must. As you are able, take time to read the long stories of the Bible. By doing so, you can get swept up into the drama of God's redemptive work, of His self-disclosure, and of His great love for us. So take your time. Settle in and read the extended passages when you are able.

Study Together

One way to study comprehensively is to study with others who are like-minded. The discipline of study should not be limited to individual application. If you doubt that, think about who received the books and letters of the Scriptures first. Only five books were addressed to individuals: Luke and Acts (Theopilus) and 1 and 2 Timothy and Titus. All of the books were intended for the people of God to encounter as a group. Private study is important, but studying together offers more spiritual insights.

Studying together can include four elements: reading, discussion, application and accountability (two sides of a coin), and service.

Read Together

Believers can read the Scripture together in two different ways. First, they can have the same reading plan. It is a powerful thought to wake up on a Thursday and know that you have friends in the faith who are diving into the same passage of Isaiah that you are. Carrying the knowledge that you are collectively mining the depth of the Bible together in preparation for a later discussion will encourage you on the journey. It will also keep you committed to the collective journey with other believers.

Another way to read together is to do so out loud. Whenever I teach university courses involving the Bible, one discipline that I engage students in is the public reading of the Bible. In one survey of the Old Testament class, I had several students tell me that it was the first time they had read the Bible aloud. I wanted their experience to mirror that of the original receivers of the Word: verbal and auditory. The Bible was meant to be heard aloud in a group. Reading it out loud allows you to hear the emotion and inflection of each passage.

Discuss the Passage

The Bible stands on its own, but we are not meant to live it out on our own. You need the work that the Holy Spirit is doing in the lives of other people. As He works in you and others, the Spirit is active in the community of faith. Plus, we all have questions. When we encounter passages that are difficult to understand or you wonder about the application, it is with fellow believers that we can gain discernment. By submitting ourselves to the power of the community, it also guards us from heresy. As we look back in history at the errant views of our faith, they often came from a person who chose to study in utter isolation. We need the church in our study of the Scriptures.

Application and Accountability

Once we read and study the Word together, help is required to obey it. When you study together, it is a natural next step to find ways to apply what we've learned. Taking this step together ensures that your application of Scripture is both personal and missional in nature. If all of our study is done alone, then we will likely only think about how the Word applies to us in a personal way. When we look for applications together as friends, then we can point our attention toward how the Word affects all of us.

Whenever you drive, you must pay attention to your blind spots. They are the places to the sides of your car where you cannot see even with mirrors, so you must turn your head to see. When you're driving, you can't just change lanes recklessly. Rather, you've got to check your blind spot to make sure another car is not there. Applying the Bible in community will also help with your spiritual blind spots. Friends can warn you of a possible disaster through loving accountability. And you can do the same for them as well.

SERVE TOGETHER

Studying the Bible should always result in a response. So as you move into application, it becomes an opportunity to serve others. As you learn what God is teaching you through the Scriptures, find a way to serve others because of it. In doing so together, it helps us to gain courage and to live out the body of Christ images in 1 Corinthians. God never designed for us to serve alone. Rather, when we learn together, we grow together, and then we can better serve the world together.

FROM THE HEAD TO THE HEART TO THE WORLD: TAKING BIBLE TRUTHS TO OTHERS

"What's true for you is not true for me."

The study of the Bible includes our brain but should not stop with it. As I mentioned earlier, I'm a bit of an information junkie. But instead of trying to be the smartest person in the room, I have found a better way. I am finding joy in letting everyone else in on what I know while seeking to learn from what others have already mastered.

It happens when you move biblical truth from your brain to the rest of your life. It is in the application of truth that we understand God's power. But specifically, I think it is the application that leads to mission. As we encounter God in the pages of the Bible, it should drive us to introduce the rest of the world to Him.

Today much of society views morality and truth as relative. "What's true for you is not true for me," many of your friends may say. Others argue, "That's fine if you want to live by those standards." But truth by its very definition is the standard. When we find ourselves in an age that has thrown off all boundary markers, we should talk about what matters most. The very nature of the Bible is that God is communicating to us. As His ambassadors, we must now do that communicating on His behalf.

Getting Involved with the Nones and the Dones

Two groups in our culture need special attention: the Nones and the Dones. The Nones are those who claim no religious affiliation. It is a growing group that includes atheists, agnostics, and those who just don't think about it. The Dones are those who once attended church and then something happened. Whether through pain, abuse, or plain disenchantment, they decided to be done with religion. So they left. The Bible is for both of these groups, but we must engage them in healthy conversations.

When talking with the Nones, our conversation will begin with finding common ground of where truth originates. When dealing with the Dones, it will mean finding the point of their disconnection to spiritual topics. With both, discussing the Bible in a way that is natural is key. They need to see that your interest in the Bible is not a passing fad or that of a lunatic.

Rather, in your best thinking, you've searched the Scriptures and found them to be authoritative. Among the Nones and Dones, most are not looking to reject truth; they just haven't found anything compelling yet.

Seeking the Unchurched, De-churched, and Antichurched

Plenty of others in our cities need to encounter the Word as well. There are the unchurched, the de-churched, and the antichurched. Everyone who is intentionally or unintentionally disengaged from a church family has made a choice. They have decided that the revelation from God—the Bible—and being in church to hear it, are unimportant. We need to learn how to talk with them. It cannot be the thunderous preacher on the street corner. Rather, it is the chance to talk friend-to-friend about the most important issue of our lives. As people of faith, at our core we believe that God has revealed Himself to us in the Bible. To go for years without ever bringing that up is beyond silly. It is ridiculous. Even more so, it is cruel.

God has revealed Himself so that all of humanity would hear from Him. Not just the select few of us who attend worship services, own a Bible, and read it for personal gain. The Scriptures, God's revealed Word, are for everyone. We must dig into it so we can grow up in it. Then as we grow up in it, we can reach out because of it. In the second to the last book of the Bible, Jude wrote to a troubled church about the need to fend off those who were twisting the truth of God's revelation. He closed his one-chapter letter with these words:

> But you, dear friends, as you build yourselves up in your most holy faith and pray in the Holy Spirit, keep

yourselves in the love of God, expecting the mercy of our Lord Jesus Christ for eternal life. Have mercy on those who doubt; save others by snatching them from the fire; have mercy on others but with fear, hating even the garment defiled by the flesh.

Now to Him who is able to protect you from stumbling and to make you stand in the presence of His glory, blameless and with great joy to the only God our Savior, through Jesus Christ our Lord, be glory, majesty, power, and authority before all time, now and forever. Amen. (vv. 20–25)

The impact of the passage on me is so clear. Grow up so I can reach out. Reach out so I can grow up. These two activities are linked, never to be separated. When we live like this, then we can fully understand the beauty Jude describes in verses 24–25. Growth and mission are the twin crucibles that God brings us through to make us look like Jesus. He is totally able and willing to shape our lives so we can stand in the gospel's power. And when we do, it brings great joy—to us, and more importantly, to Him, the only God our Savior.

Today, take great joy in the gift of God's Word.

Chapter 4

THE GREAT CONVERSATION:

THE PRACTICE OF PRAYER

Worship, Bible study, and prayer are the three foundational disciplines of the Christian life.

We worship in order to communicate the worthiness of God, to proclaim the greatness of the one true God. As we study the Word, we learn from God about who He is, who we are, and how He is reconciling all things to Himself. Then, when we come to prayer, we move to a specifically intimate interaction with God. So let us consider the practice of prayer.

To properly practice prayer, we need to understand its nature. For many, prayer is simply offering a laundry list of needs to God. Others consider it a time for confession that in and of itself will require God to in turn offer forgiveness. In non-Christian faith traditions, prayer is often a practice of repetitious phrases that will please the deity. Prayer, however, is much more than merely rattling off whatever is on the top of our minds or repeating phrases with great passion.

DEFINING PRAYER

Many books—and I mean many—have been written on the subject of prayer. In them, you can find all kinds of definitions. Here are a few:

- Climbing up to the heart of God (Martin Luther).
- Talking with God who listens and responds because He loves us (Fisher Humphreys).
- Divine communication with God (Dick Eastman).
- To pray is to change (Richard Foster).
- True, whole prayer is nothing but love (St. Augustine).

These definitions offer a poetic feeling toward prayer. They give a sense that prayer is more about love than it is about obligation. As you are moving through this personal, communal, and missional journey on the spiritual disciplines, keep in mind that love must remain at the heart of why we engage in these spiritual activities. Prayer certainly is an activity that is more delight than it is duty.

From the beginning of human history, we find that the Lord has spoken. At the creation of Adam and subsequently Eve, God spoke to them. Even when they rebelled for the first time, God came to them and spoke, asking where Adam was. It is God who initiates our relationship with Him and He speaks to us. As we've seen in the previous chapter, God has spoken authoritatively through the Scriptures. In prayer, by virtue of the indwelling of the Holy Spirit with believers, we have God's presence with us to prompt us with His discernment and wisdom. Romans 8:16 states, "The Spirit Himself testifies together with our spirit that we are God's children." The Greek word for "testifies together with" means to corroborate or bear witness.

It is my conviction that God has authoritatively and infallibly spoken through the Bible. In terms of our relationship with Him now, it is the presence of His Spirit who moves in us and teaches us to understand the Word. With prayer, we can realistically understand it as communication with God as a response to His initiatives. Poetically, prayer is our response to the echoes of Eden where we long to walk with God in the cool of the day. To state it as simply as possible, prayer is two-way communication that is initiated by His love.

THE COMMUNICATION GAP

Why do human relationships break down? Often it's because of a communication gap. We forget to adequately listen to and speak clearly to family members and friends. It may be an issue of ego: Certain that we are speaking clearly enough for everyone to understand us, we fail to listen to them. Focused on our own needs, we endlessly chatter on about our personal lives. In contrast, when our relationships are healthy, we become attentive listeners.

In marriage, a lack of healthy communication is often the culprit when a relationship goes sour. With my wife, Angie, often I am tempted to walk in the room, rattle off a list of needs, and expect her to meet each one. After all, she's my wife and loves me. Right? Of course she does. But it is disrespectful and devaluing to her when I demand her service but never give her my love. Instead, my conversations should be a way for me to love her by listening, heeding her calls to action, and responding with the heart of a servant.

The same communication gap is why we desperately need the right view on prayer. Without properly understanding this spiritual discipline, we will lapse into abusing our relationship with God. In our immaturity, prayer too often is about getting our point across to God rather than coming under His loving hand. We hold up our needs in an arrogant fashion and demand to be His priority. Our prayers border on self-idolatry when we displace God from the throne so we can ascend to His position. This sinful and disjointed view of our salvation places self at the center of God's kingdom.

In treating prayer as a spiritual discipline, we learn to respond to the loving activity of the Father. In prayer, I tell Christ of my love for Him and ask for the Spirit's filling so I can obey the will of the Father. In bowing my will before God in prayer, I show my deep love for all He has done and will do. Even more, prayer is the moment that I declare my love for God in the most intimate of circumstances.

THE ELEMENTS OF PRAYER

In regard to the basic parts of prayer, I want to focus on confession, intercession, and petition as broad categories. Not to skip the issues of worship and thanksgiving, I'll point you back to chapter 2 for applying worship into your prayer life.

Confession

During our prayers, confession is the *admission of our sin and the desire for restoration* of our relationship with God. Psalm

51 is understood to be the prayer of confession by King David after his adulterous affair with Bathsheba and murder of her husband, Uriah. The prayer is a cry for help because of the devastation brought about by sin. In our confession, we learn to lean upon God's character in order to find God's forgiveness. Like David, we can pray, "Be gracious to me, God, according to Your faithful love; according to Your abundant compassion, blot out my rebellion" (v. 1).

Our confession must also *recognize who we have offended*. David has committed adultery and had a man killed on the battlefield. Yet in his prayer, he said to the Lord, "Against You—You alone—I have sinned and done this evil in Your sight" (v. 4). David was aware of his sin and knew that it was against God's holiness that it was committed. As we enter into confession, we will be aware of the pain our sin has caused other people and, at the right opportunity, we should seek reconciliation with others. But let's remember that all sin is primarily a crime against God's holiness.

Confession is also *a discipline by the church*. It is the place where we need to move from routine church prayer lists of recurring needs to the church praying about apathy toward holiness and ignoring God's mission. Is there anything wrong with a church prayer list? In and of itself, no. We should and must pray for our friends who are sick, carrying grief, and in need of our petitions before God. But those outward-facing prayers must not be the sum

> *Prayer should drive us to a sense of God's work in both us and the world around us.*

total of how a church prays. Rather, a church must be found praying often—and concerning sin quite often.

Many of the Old Testament examples of God's people in prayer concern Israel's sin. They would collectively cry out to God to forgive their sins. The songs of confession we find in the book of Psalms were used by groups of people. Similarly we must readily admit when our congregation, small group, or even family have entered into sin.

One potential area of collective sin that you can examine is favoritism of people in certain classes or races. The charge leveled years ago that 11:00 on Sunday mornings is the most segregated hour in America remains true for many, if not most, churches. If a church finds that a discriminatory attitude exists, then corporate confession is appropriate. It is in prayer that the Holy Spirit can more deeply apply the Scriptures to our lives. Prayer should drive us to a sense of God's work in both us and the world around us. As such, in prayer, a church family can turn away from any sin and better follow after God's heart.

The prayer of confession by a group of people must be handled carefully. For some, they have actively engaged in sin together. Others have turned a blind eye to it. Then there are those who sought to stop sin and call the church back to the Lord. In all of this, it requires godly leadership to help the church navigate properly through times of confession. Our goal is for the guilty to learn the beauty of confession and the innocent to encourage those who are reconciling their relationships.

Intercession

Intercessory prayer is the work that we do of bringing someone else's needs before the throne of God. In fact, intercessory prayer is a very God-like activity. After all, the Incarnation itself is the work done by the Son to place the needs of humanity before His own. In ministry and in death, He interceded by action.

Now, we are told in Hebrews 7:25 about Jesus' current ministry in heaven. "Therefore, He is always able to save those who come to God through Him, since He always lives to intercede for them." The apostle Paul wrote, "Christ Jesus is the One who died, but even more, has been raised; He also is at the right hand of God and intercedes for us" (Rom. 8:34). Apparently, this is an important work for Jesus. As His disciples, we participate with Him by interceding for those around us.

Intercession can be understood as letting go of my own neediness for the sake of God's work in another's life. It does not require ignoring self but prioritizing others. Intercessory prayer allows us to better imitate Christ by choosing a servant posture as He did. It also teaches us perseverance. In Luke 18:1–8, Jesus told the story of a persistent widow who kept asking the town judge for justice. She would not give up with her requests until he relented. In the parable, Jesus is teaching us perseverance as we wait on God to move in His perfect timing. We must not give up even if the answer does not arrive immediately.

Intercession also requires a life of personal holiness. As you commit to intercessory prayer, you must also commit to having a life set apart for God's purposes. Peter tells us the church is a "royal priesthood" (1 Peter 2:9). It's a role to take with sober joy. We are happy to hold up the needs of others before the omnipotent God. But we do so with an understanding of what is required to stand before Him.

As a pastor, I've been in many meetings of intercessory prayer. These gatherings have a steady diet of praying for the physical needs and illnesses of people. Periodically, we would also pray for a family in financial need. But we need to expand our thinking about intercessory prayer. We can intercede beyond the realm of the physical needs. That is what the first-century church did. They prayed for one another's spiritual maturity, for boldness in the midst of governmental persecution (see Acts 29), and for the lost to be saved.

As you pray, do it the right way. Establish your purpose. Seek the grace of God so that fellowship with God and usefulness with God will be established and maintained. Then address the problem. Intercession is not wishful thinking for your friends. It is directly addressing the issues of suffering and/or sin in a life. Then, we can present our plea. As we walk intimately with Jesus, we should make our requests to God. It is not outside the boundary markers to actually ask God for a specific outcome. If you are walking closely with the Lord then He is providing the discernment for you to learn what to ask. Finally, we must wait patiently. Praying with faith provides the opportunity for us all to grow in faith as we wait in faith.

Intercessory prayer must go beyond reciting a grocery list of needs and praying for family, close friends, and other people we like. Our work is to seek God's role in the lives of our friends—and enemies too. If you will commit yourself to a life of intercessory prayer, you will enter into beautiful territory with the people around you. For many of your friends, neighbors, coworkers, and people you might meet on the mission field, your offer to pray for their needs will be the first time it has ever occurred in their lives. You may be the first person they know who was willing to place his or her own needs aside and lift their needs to the heavenly Father.

Petition

Worship is when we talk to God about God. Intercession is when we talk to God about others. Petition is when we talk to God about ourselves. James wrote, "You ask and don't receive because you ask with wrong motives, so that you may spend it on your evil desires" (4:3). The lesson is that it is not just okay but expected for us to ask God to meet our needs. The great British preacher Charles Spurgeon once said, "Asking is the rule of the Kingdom." It is a phrase I have embraced.

Petitionary prayer does not give us the permission to simply name what we want and think that we have obligated God to provide it. Otherwise, we'd all be independently wealthy and some pageant contestant would have the world hunger problem solved by now. No, our prayers of petition must be lifted in a very specific ethic: it is in the name of Jesus that we make our requests known before God. We don't come with a demand that God open the treasure chests of heaven. Rather, we come before Him with an open heart to receive the good gifts He has chosen to give us.

In Acts 4:23–31 the early church gives us a framework on how to make our petitions to God. After Peter and John were released from prison, the church's first order of business was to gather for prayer. They began in verses 24–25 with praise, referring to God's sovereignty, creative power, and desire to reveal Himself to humanity. Worship gives us the right attitude to ask for the right things. By recognizing God as our source, we can then gladly receive any answer He offers.

Then they allowed the Scriptures to give perspective to their request. In verses 25–26, they quoted from Psalm 2 as a reminder that nothing is new to God. Every time we bring a need, He has seen it before. By engaging biblical material in our prayer life, we assure ourselves of God's perspective of our needs.

They then analyzed their circumstances in light of past circumstances. They remembered that their persecution should be seen in light of what Christ has already done and God's presence with them (vv. 27–28). By analyzing our problems properly, it aids us in avoiding shallowness and, may I add, becoming whiny children. By doing such, we can base our petition on our wills and not on our wishes. We want to be intentional. After all, some children spend more time deciding what they will ask Santa Claus for Christmas than we usually spend before making our petitions to God. We need to show God the respect of a well-considered request.

Once we have carefully considered the circumstances, it is time to make our petition. They prayed, "And now, Lord, consider their threats, and grant that Your slaves may speak Your message with complete boldness, while You stretch out Your hand for healing, signs, and wonders to be performed through the name of Your holy Servant Jesus" (vv. 29–30). The request was simple. After all, God never demanded us to be eloquent. The believers' prayer addressed their needs but was in greater measure for God's glory to be made known. Even in our petitions, we must keep God's glory in mind.

Finally, as the church experienced in verse 31, we can expect God to answer. For them, it was the presence and filling of the Holy Spirit. For us, it can be that and more. Through this whole process, God is not just looking to fix a problem for you

THE GREAT CONVERSATION: THE PRACTICE OF PRAYER

but to reveal Himself to you in greater measure. He wants you to know Him and His purposes in your life.

In December 2000, our son Chris was three months shy of his third birthday. At a store, we asked him what he wanted for Christmas. His eyes fell on the giant cage of rubber balls. They were all bigger than him. His answer was "a big, yellow ball!" When Angie returned later to buy the big, yellow ball . . . they were all gone. The store only had big, red balls. So, what we had for Chris and what he wanted were in competition with one another. We spent the next few weeks convincing Chris that what he wanted was a red ball, not a yellow ball.

So it is good that this is not a book about parenting. But I think you get the message. We had to convince him of what he wanted based on what his parents were going to give him as a gift. The illustration breaks down but I hope the idea does not. God has great answers for us. It guides me to this idea: The very first thing we should ask of God is what we should ask of God.

Petitionary prayer has been derided at times as too selfish. When it becomes the only type of prayer we offer, the critique is well founded. But God obviously expects and even requires us to ask for His intervention in our personal circumstances of life. As with any earthly relationship, it would be odd if you never, ever spoke about your own life. We must remember that God enjoys us and cares deeply about the details of our lives.

THE VOLUME OF SILENCE

When we love someone, we listen to what the person has to say. Yet prayer is most often considered to be a time of speaking. We need to learn to be quiet before the Lord so that

He has relational space to guide us. Silence in prayer is your submission before God, allowing Him to have the first and last words on any subject and any part of your life. It is necessary in order to curb our childlike tendency to speak before we think. The teacher in Ecclesiastes 5:2, says, "Do not be hasty to speak, and do not be impulsive to make a speech before God. God is in your heaven and you are on earth, so let your words be few."

The silence in our prayers takes on many forms. It is a time of watching. When Jesus went to the garden of Gethsemane, He asked the apostles to watch and pray. It is the sense that we pray with insight, understanding the world around us—and, as Jesus warned, guarding against temptation (Mark 14:38). Rather than just pray for whatever comes to the top of our mind, we watch what is occurring around us in the world and allow the Spirit to inform us of how to pray.

Waiting is spoken of in Zechariah 2:13. The prophet said, "Let all people be silent before the Lord, for He is coming from His holy dwelling." The psalmist said, "Be still, and know that I am God" (Ps. 46:10 NIV). When we pray, we should do so in a posture of faith knowing that God is moving. Because He is working and we are responding, volumes of words are unnecessary. The act of waiting shows that I love God and His activity more than I need Him to see my own. I love waiting for the Spirit to teach me how to apply the Scriptures to my life. In the silent waiting, loving faith is expressed and strengthened.

In Mark 11:22, Jesus said to the crowds, "Have faith in God." When we choose to be silent, patient, and wait, we are expressing our faith in God, not in prayer. Prayer is the tool that He uses to give us space to mature. As the people of God, we should do the same. Our prayer times as a small group or a congregation should not be filled with endless phrases or meaningless repetitions from the last prayer time. Instead, we should embrace the silence of prayer together. As we watch, we pray. As we pray, we wait. Rather than leaning on our own understanding to cast a vision, church leaders and all Christians should listen to the directives from the Spirit. This is where we can show our love and faith. It is where we are set apart for His holy cause.

PRAYER AS THE MISSION

Prayer should bring about a sense of God's mission. It is because of the world's spiritually lost condition that we pray for God's intervention. As we pray, we should do so for our needs yet subjugate those personal needs below the global need for redemption.

Your prayers can turn missional when you seek for God's kingdom to reign in the hearts of those living in your community. We should intercede for the physical needs of others. Asking God to provide food, shelter, and safety to widows, orphans, and immigrants is a noble and missionary request. Letting go of your own wish list of needs and putting someone else's first will better shape your heart to love people as Jesus loves them. It is this building of faith that will further propel us into the world. In lifting up a need for a fellow human being and then being silent long enough to understand the Spirit's guidance, it is likely that He will send you into the work of filling that need. Prayer is not a separate spiritual discipline from God's mission. Prayer informs us of our role in His mission.

By bearing down in prayer, we learn to persevere in faith.

All of us have experienced the waiting necessary for an answer to a request made before the Father. He is not unreliable or ignoring us when we do not receive provisions immediately. Circumstances are provided in such a way to give room for faith and love to grow. It is by this same faith and love that we will be propelled into the mission field of God's choosing. As individuals and congregations learn to persevere in prayer, persevering in ministry will become more natural for us.

Here's one very practical way that prayer works in the mission of God. As you interact with people in your community—or on a foreign mission trip—you will have the opportunity to pray *with* those you meet. Notice that I wrote "with" and not "for." In the moments of ministry to the poor and needy or wealthy and well-supplied, we often are tempted to say, "I'll pray for you about [fill in the blank of their need and/or wish list before God]." A more effective route is to ask the person if you can pray *with* them at that moment. With billions of people on the planet who are not believers, praying with them is a missionary activity. You likely have people in your own neighborhood or apartment complex for whom you will be the first person to ever pray with them. It is a privilege to not take lightly. It is a gospel moment to seize.

> *Letting go of your own wish list of needs and putting someone else's first will shape your heart to love people as Jesus does.*

A FINAL WORD

Prayer is one of the great gifts of love God bestows upon humanity. Consider the scope of its nature. Finite man speaks to the infinite God. The eternal Holy Spirit indwells believers and helps us understand the Bible. We sit quietly and wait for the Lord to direct us in His will. In prayer, we take the everyday needs of people—commonplace and severe—and lift them before the throne of the God we love. We do this because we know that He loves us.

Prayer is a deeply mysterious practice. We are heard, each one of us, by our Creator. We speak to Him because He has initiated a covenant of love with us. We tell God of our love for Him and are thereby launched into His great mission to connect others to Him in such great intimacy as well.

Chapter 5

A HUNGER FOR THE UNKNOWN:

THE PRACTICE OF FASTING

We eat. In fact, we eat a lot. At least in my country we do. Eating is how we gather the family together. Dinners are held to celebrate major milestones in life. For weddings, there is a dinner for the wedding rehearsal and a reception with food after the ceremony. At graduation parties, there is food.

It is our nature to gather around the table for the purpose of connecting with one another. Perhaps that is why the spiritual discipline of fasting seems to be such an interruption to our lives. The idea that you will voluntarily not eat for a period of time feels like an ancient practice. And that's because it is. But we should not think that the ancients felt any less strange about it.

In the time of Jesus' ministry, banquets and feasts were common as well. Going back even further, days of banqueting filled Old Testament times. Wedding celebrations would go on for days, and religious festivals often involved large dinner parties that also lasted for days. In comparison to those times, our meals may be somewhat smaller! So fasting as a practice may actually have been stranger in ancient days than it seems to be in our modern era.

Of course, eating is something we do to simply survive. It is a foundational activity, like breathing. Every day we wake up hungry. We typically eat three meals a day. For those of us living in the developed country like the United States, we have access to food throughout the day. As I write this chapter, I'm sitting in my home with a pantry filled with cans and boxes of food. There is a refrigerator with frozen meats, ice cream, sauces, and leftovers from two nights ago. I eat because I need to and, honestly, because I like to.

UNDERSTANDING THE DISCIPLINE

Eating is both for our survival and our socializing. So, when we engage in fasting as a spiritual discipline, it upsets the normal activity of life. It is unnatural because we need food and we need people. By fasting, we reveal a hunger for something that is eternal. We long to have a deeper communion with God. During fasting we willingly forgo what fuels our body to connect with the One who saves our soul.

Many Christians have never fasted. In fact, for many readers, this is the first time they have encountered any material about it. But Jesus made it clear that fasting can be a part of our lives. In Matthew 6:16, Jesus said, "Whenever you fast . . ." and then gave instructions. By neglecting this discipline, we neglect a powerful work by God in our lives. A life that is forever absent of fasting will not encounter a specific kind of testing that purifies our faith. We will miss out on how the Holy Spirit can alert us to the childish nature of our basest hunger. Refusing to fast, we will never know a deeper level of desperation that causes our soul to reach toward God, our provider of His good gifts. Fasting is hard; thus it is a discipline. But without it, we may not know how to fully satisfy our spiritual hunger.

Fasting is an interruption to your life. But understood as a spiritual discipline, it is much more. So let me offer a working definition of this activity. Fasting is a spiritual discipline that completely or partially eliminates food and/or drink in order to spend mealtimes in prayer for biblical purposes. Now, let me break it down phrase by phrase.

Fasting is a biblical practice done for kingdom purposes.

As with all that we are exploring, fasting is a *spiritual discipline*. With this activity, we place love at the heart of what we do and why we do it. But you and I must acknowledge that it requires effort. Perhaps more than many of the other disciplines, fasting takes a level of willpower we're not accustomed to exerting. For fasting, we need to take note of both words in the phrase "spiritual discipline." It requires discipline of our will. Your body will rebel against your willpower. Staying with the fast won't be easy.

Besides being a mere discipline, fasting needs to be spiritual. If you are fasting to lose weight, then you're just on a bad diet. Fasting to go along with a holiday is just moralism. Fasting must be done with your spiritual relationship to Christ in mind or it is simply a waste of your time. It is a biblical practice done for kingdom purposes. Trusting God for your body's care will of necessity increase when you fast.

In fasting, you are choosing to *completely or partially eliminate food and/or drink* for a period of time. In this, I'm going to be a bit of a stickler. At times, I've heard various believers (and a few non-believers) say that they are going on a television fast, social media fast, or some other sort of fast. My answer is that those are all worthy exercises for our souls. However, skipping your favorite shows for a week is not what the Bible describes as fasting. Only when we are denying food and/or drink to our bodies for a period of time are we fasting in the biblical sense.

Choosing the Length and Type of Fast

As you plan your fast, you must make certain decisions about how you'll go about it. Determining the length of the fast and the type of the fast should be carefully considered. (Going into a fast with an undetermined timeline is fine but you should mentally prepare yourself for that.) Also, you should decide if you will abstain from all food and all drinking. If so, you need to seek to understand the physical dynamics of abstaining from consuming zero water. (Withholding water depends on the length of the fast; see later paragraph.)

One medical warning, however. You should be aware of any physical needs. People with special dietary needs, including diabetics and those with other medical conditions, need to be cautious before skipping any meals. Consult with your physician to discuss your options regarding any of your medical conditions. If your doctor advises you against fasting, heed his or her warning. Please remember the nature of fasting. We are engaging in a spiritual activity and not a legalistic checklist.

There are no hard-and-fast rules about fasting in the Bible. There are no passages that strictly outline the logistics of fasting, such as whether you should fast for one meal, one day, or several days. It is important, then, that we remember this principle: Where God has not spoken, don't make up rules. Fasting can become, like all of the disciplines, an insidious form of legalism. It is not to earn points with God or manipulate Him. In fact, we need to keep that idea in mind as applying to all of the spiritual disciplines. In terms of fasting, the Bible describes the occurrence on a number of occasions but rarely gives prescriptive rules for it. So, let's move carefully through the process.

As you pray about entering into a fast, allow the Spirit to guide you regarding the type of fast you will do. An absolute fast eliminates all food and water. *It is done only for a short period of time*. After all, physiology catches up with you and water is a necessity after a few days before physical damage occurs. A partial fast is choosing to eliminate a particular food group or mealtime. Perhaps you choose to not eat lunch every day for a certain period of time. A standard fast is when you eliminate food and only take in liquid for a set amount of time.

No matter what type of fast you choose, I encourage you to begin it with a set time in mind and a manner of fasting. Remember to be mindful of your body's medical needs throughout the time. It is important to prepare yourself for the inevitable headaches, stomach growling, hunger pangs, and odd taste in your mouth from the experience. If it is the first time to fast, go slow. It is likely not a good idea to try to fast for one week your first time.

Keeping a Spiritual Focus

As we fast, it is *appropriate to spend what would have been our mealtimes in prayer*. Remember, without prayer, you are just on a bad diet. It is a time of refusing earthly sustenance in order to gain a greater desire for Christ. The whole point of the disciplines is to express our love to God and experience His love for us. So, we don't just eliminate food as a show of willpower. Rather, we engage God with the time that would have been spent eating. Personally, when I fast, my intention is to spend the time necessary for preparation, eating, and cleanup as time devoted to prayer.

As we eliminate mealtimes for prayer, we need to ensure that our prayers are for *biblical purposes*. Again, there are no set-in-stone categories for fasting in the Bible. However, we have numerous descriptions of why people entered into seasons of fasting. It has normally been associated with seeking God's help in the face of calamity, temptation, or making a major decision. We'll look more at a few specific instances in the next section.

Again, the definition we're using to understand this discipline is: Fasting is a spiritual discipline that completely or partially eliminates food and/or drink in order to spend your mealtimes in prayer for biblical purposes. Think about it from a personal perspective: fasting has the potential to focus your attention more closely on God's Word and work in you. But, as we see in all of the disciplines, fasting affects the church community as well. Now let's take a look at why we should enter into such a practice.

MOTIVATIONS FOR FASTING

To Establish God-Centered Living

Why would anyone willfully choose *not* to eat? Just the thought of it sounds unhelpful at best and a bit of lunacy at worst. But there are serious spiritual motivations involved for fasting. The *first motivation for fasting is to better establish God-centered living.* Consider God's words to the prophet Zechariah: "Then the word of the Lord of Hosts came to me: 'Ask all the people of the land and the priests: When you fasted and lamented in the fifth and in the seventh months for these 70 years, did you really fast for Me?'" (7:4–5).

God is asking the Israelites if they fasted for the purpose of knowing the Lord or for some other reason. "Did you really fast for Me?" is the haunting question that should linger with us. God's question to the people in Zechariah dovetails well with Isaiah 58:1–5, where God is again testing the people's motives for fasting. Sadly, in the Isaiah passage, God reveals that their purpose of fasting was hypocritical and simply done out of religious ritual.

The fasting that will please God is an activity that draws us closer to a knowledge of Him and an obedience to His will. As Jesus preached during the Sermon on the Mount, "Whenever you fast, don't be sad-faced like the hypocrites. For they make their faces unattractive so their fasting is obvious to people. I assure you: They've got their reward! But when you fast, put oil on your head, and wash your face, so that you don't show your fasting to people but to your Father who is in secret. And your Father who sees in secret will reward you" (Matt. 6:16–18). Our fasting is not to extend our religious reputation in and out of the church. Its primary purpose is to fully focus our attention on the God who sustains and guides us through every circumstance of life. So, keep your focus on God throughout the fast.

To Reveal What Controls Us

Second, fasting reveals what controls us. The moment we deny food to our body, it reveals something about us. It proves how powerful and clever our body is at getting its own way against our strongest resolve.

Fasting is the place in your life where the war against the flesh becomes its most real. I've thought about it this way: Financial generosity battles against our means of existence. Prayer battles against our need to control our time. Fasting battles against our self-reliance. You must scour your belly empty by hunger to learn that man does not live by bread alone. But in doing so, your belly will rebel.

Food is convenient. Fasting is not. Eating is the cultural norm. Fasting sets you apart as different. Food brings about physical pleasure. Fasting introduces us to a time of physical discomfort. Eating is done out of absolute necessity. Fasting is done out of absolute faith.

When you fast, you ask God to reveal a deep truth about your own soul. It shows that your stomach is a whiny child revolting at the moment it is denied the most unnecessary morsel of food. It is in these moments that you can willfully decide that your physical condition will not control the condition of your soul. It is certainly here that the "discipline" of "spiritual discipline" must take root. We learn that so much stuff of earth holds sway over our happiness, decision-making, and attitude toward ministry. Fasting is a beautiful test of what or Who rules our lives.

To Confirm Our Dependence on God

Third, fasting will confirm our dependence on God. After Jesus fasted for forty days, He was obviously hungry. So Satan began the first of his three temptations of Jesus by offering to satisfy His hunger by supernatural means. As with all three of the temptations, Jesus answered Satan with Scripture. Quoting Deuteronomy 8:3, Jesus declared, "Man must not live on bread alone but on every word that comes from the mouth of God" (Matt. 4:4).

In this moment, the Son of God shows us the example of what dependence upon the Father must be. It must be absolute. It must be complete.

In John 4, Jesus was again faced with the pangs of hunger. As He traveled with His disciples, they encouraged Him to eat. Though this is not an instance of fasting, the principle applies well for us in it. Rather than eat, Jesus said, "I have food to eat that you don't know about. . . . My food is to do the will of Him who sent Me and to finish His work" (John 4:32, 34).

This attitude from Jesus is often a foreign concept in our own lives. I feel like having a snack about every two hours. Do I yearn for God the same way? My attitude should be that I feast on the presence and work of God. In the Christian's life, there should be a holy hunger for God that overshadows all other desires. Fasting disciplines our bodies so that the proper hunger remains front and center.

During Jesus' earthly ministry, the disciples of John the Baptist questioned why Jesus' disciples did not fast. Jesus' answer used the imagery of a wedding feast. "Can the wedding guests be sad while the groom is with them? The time will come when the groom will be taken away from them, and then they will fast" (Matt. 9:15). It is the time in which we live. We fast because we need the presence of the Groom. As the church, we are a bride who eagerly awaits His return. Until then, we fast at times for our relational connection to Christ.

FASTING IN BIBLE TIMES

Let me reiterate that where God has not made a rule, we should not make up our own set of rules. Instead, we can look confidently toward the Bible and better understand why God's people have fasted in the past. From there, we can determine proper reasons to do it now.

Reasons to Fast from Isaiah

In Isaiah 58:6–9, we read this word from God:

"Isn't the fast I choose: To break the chains of wickedness, to untie the ropes of the yoke, to set the oppressed free, and to tear off every yoke? Is it not to share your bread with the hungry, to bring the poor and homeless into your house, to clothe the naked when you see him, and not to ignore your own flesh and blood? Then your light will appear like the dawn, and your recovery will come quickly. Your righteousness will go before you, and the Lord's glory will be your rear guard. At that time, when you call, the Lord will answer; when you cry out, He will say, 'Here I am.'"

The passage gives numerous reasons for fasting. The language of breaking chains, untying ropes, setting oppressed people free, and tearing apart yokes gives a very certain meaning. Fasting can be a time to break a sin's hold on us. Through denial of earthly pleasure through food, we can more pointedly rely on God's presence to satisfy us. Then, sin's illusion of satisfaction is laid bare for us to see. The denial we make to the body reveals the deception of sin's temptations. As we more closely focus on God during our fast, we find His sustaining work in us to be more joyous than anything the world or the enemy can offer.

Fasting can also be a time to care for the needy. In verse 7, we are told that during the fast, we can welcome others into our lives to receive what we are denying to ourselves. In the time Isaiah's prophecy was delivered, it was the cue for the Israelites to care for their countrymen while in exile. At the time of fasting, you may choose to give food, shelter, and clothing to the poor. There is even a reminder to not ignore your own family. Fasting is denying ourselves these things and opens a missional opportunity for a kind of compassion that we're not likely to show otherwise.

Fasting is a time that results in intimacy and public witness . . . and a time of seeking God's protection.

Fasting is a time to allow God's reputation and glory to characterize us. The discipline focuses our attention on relying on God for our needs, happiness, and self-worth. It is a time that results in intimacy with the Father. The Bible also shows fasting as a time of seeking God's protection. The rear guard has military connotations. In fasting you may be seeking God as your defense against life's disasters or in the midst of spiritual warfare. So often, we only consider fasting as a privatized experience. However, it is nearly impossible for not eating to go unnoticed by others. So, it becomes a time to humbly display that God is at work in your life.

Fasting also gives you an opportunity to receive an answer from the Lord. In verse 9, He said, "At that time, when you call, the Lord will answer; when you cry out, He will say, 'Here I am.'" Remember, when we fast, it is to seek God, not to discipline ourselves out of gluttonous behavior. During a time of fasting, we bring our needs before God. The prophet delivered the message that we are to cry out to Him for an answer. Fasting is not a time to be timid. During it, be bold. Ask God for answers. Seek Him for power. It is a time for our deep desire for being filled with the Holy Spirit to be expressed to Him.

Fasting during Calamity

Beyond the Isaiah passage, there are numerous places in the Bible that describe the people of God fasting. In 2 Samuel 1, news is brought to David that King Saul and his son Jonathan had died in battle. At the news, David and his men all tore their clothes as a sign of mourning and then fasted. It is an example of fasting during times of calamity. All of us will face tragedy and disaster. What we do in response to it unveils a great deal about our faith. In facing the loss of the king and his best friend, David fasted. When you and I are facing loss in our family, at work, or even in the death of a close friend, fasting can be a spiritual discipline that will anchor our perspective back to God's unwavering presence in our lives.

Fasting during Confession of Sin

The confession of sin is another opportunity for fasting. In both 2 Samuel 12 and Nehemiah 9, we read of God's people fasting while they navigate through a time of confession and repentance. In 2 Samuel 12, the prophet Nathan reminds King David of his adultery with Bathsheba and the king's instruction that caused Uriah, Bathsheba's husband, to die in battle. At being confronted with the consequences of his sin, David enters a time of prayer and fasting that leads him toward repentance.

In Nehemiah 9, many of the Hebrews have returned from exile to resettle Jerusalem. However, they squandered much of their time there until Nehemiah arrived. Upon the completion of rebuilding the walls around Jerusalem, Ezra the high priest then brings out the Law of God and reestablishes the covenant with the people. In response, they enter a time of fasting to confess their national sins and turn their lives back to the Lord. These two biblical examples show us fasting in response to sin on both a private and a community level.

Fasting to Worship God

Fasting is also an act of worship in and of itself. In Acts 13, the church members in the city of Antioch are described as "ministering to the Lord and fasting" (v. 2) when the Holy Spirit spoke to them. Though fasting is often associated with negative circumstances such as confession, tragedy, or needing God's answer to a dire situation, in Acts 13 we see a different reason for it. Fasting is a form of worship. For the early believers, they were likely seeking God's power for ministry. After all, they lived in the hostile environment of the Roman Empire.

But it is a powerful example to us that believers sometimes fast simply to focus more closely on worshiping God.

Fasting to Choose Leaders

A final example of fasting we can point to is found in the very next chapter of Acts. Once Paul and his devoted associate Barnabas had gone through the areas of Lystra and Iconium, they returned to Antioch, which was now the proverbial home base of the church. They prayed and fasted to commission the newly appointed elders of the churches (Acts 14:23).

In this passage and in numerous places throughout church history, fasting has been a practice in the process of choosing new leaders for the church. It is such a critical decision that it certainly warrants the type of attention that fasting brings into our prayer lives. Paul and the early leaders did not send the new elders to their places of service without this type of intense prayer.

Finally, fasting reminds us that we need God's wisdom for commissioning leaders. It is not just a passing idea in Acts that leaders were chosen through times of intense fasting and prayer. When a church is in need of leadership, it must first look to the Lord and not to the person who seems most qualified by worldly standards. Israel did that once and they got King Saul because of it. In the church, we are relying on Christ as our King and the Holy Spirit's indwelling power for discerning the right choice.

As you can see, the reasons for fasting run the gamut of human experience. It is for times of both need and worship. We can fast when we need to repent or when we know that temptation is on the horizon. As we seek to understand when to fast, the Bible gives us no concrete rules. Rather, it is the discipline that we do when our hearts need to be drawn more closely to God's provision rather than our sustenance and cleverness.

FASTING IN COMMUNITY

Fasting has been most often taught as a private discipline. And it is an act calling for personal humility. Even Jesus taught this idea, as He told the disciples to act normally while fasting, not drawing attention to the fact that they were doing it. Those who did show off so people would notice had gained all the reward they would ever receive (see Matt. 6:16–18). God had rebuked Israel for fasting to be seen rather than to bow before God (Zech. 7:5–7).

Yet those cautions do not mean that fasting is always to be done in isolation. Many of the examples we've looked at involve groups of people. As believers, fasting is a practice that can greatly strengthen our relationships with one another. Rather than allowing ourselves to remain at the proverbial surface level, we must be committed to another person's spiritual well-being to enter a fast with them. It becomes a powerful testimony to friendship and ministry to each other when you skip meals as friends, a small group, or an entire church for the purpose of crying out to God for help and comfort.

Fasting focuses the worship of the church. As noted earlier, the first-century church fasted as they ministered before the Lord. Consider what might occur if your church family committed itself to a time of fasting; to plainly say, "We love You, Lord, and trust You completely." It is the type of discipline that places love at the center of our lives. Rather than trying to be busy for God, we simply love God for His sustaining power.

Entering a fast together encourages accountability. We are more sly, clever, and deceitful than we want to admit. And we cheat at stuff all of the time. In a corporate fast, we invite other believers to hold us accountable to the time of commitment. When your resolve weakens, you have others to rely on and vice versa. The accountability is not there to play a spiritual game of "Gotcha" but to encourage each other toward complete faith in God.

Fasting relieves the church from thinking that it can grow by cleverness. Fasting will strip away every idea that we are in control of what happens next. When we fast, we give up on the quick-fix remedies for church growth, like planning an impressive schedule of upcoming events. Instead, we joyfully jump into the arms of our heavenly Father and declare again that He is all we need. It can be a declaration by a married couple raising kids, friends facing hard times, or an entire church to say to God, "Only You can make and develop disciples. We trust You to do it through us as we're obedient to Your Word." Fasting moves us quickly from self-reliance to a posture of faith.

As noted earlier and practiced by the early church (Acts 14:23), in choosing leaders who are most qualified the church today must first look to the Lord and not to the worldly standards. This is aided by fasting. Indeed, choosing church leaders is a process worthy of fasting so that greater focus can be achieved and complete faith can be expressed. As a church, it is a wise idea to fast prior to choosing leaders.

A WITNESS TO THE WORLD AND A REVEALER TO US

Much of the work resulting from fasting is seen as internal. We are made more holy by confession and repentance. Wisdom is gained from God because of the intensity of our prayer times. We are able to better understand how God is calling His people to live. But all of this has an outward effect.

Fasting itself becomes a witness to the world. People who are not of the faith will question your motives and ask if you are somehow obligating God to bless you. It is an opportunity to once again say that we fast as a response to grace, not to earn it.

Fasting will also reveal what part of our lives is getting in the way of the missional task ahead of us. Fasting reveals moodiness, selfish behavior, and what sets off our anger. Hunger will do that to you. When we understand that our appetites are like children who demand our total attention, it gives an opportunity for the Spirit to show us what is controlling us. The act of fasting reveals what we love the most. Sadly, some find out that they actually do love food more than anything else. For others, our heart's affections are shown to be on a multitude of things rather than on Christ. When our hearts are put back in order, then we can see our way more clearly to participating in God's mission to redeem the lost and care for the hurting.

Finally, too many of us simply don't know what to do next regarding God's mission in the world. We involve ourselves in the ministries of our church and find a level of satisfaction that is real but not complete. It is a signal that we need to pray more earnestly for God's direction. Fasting is the discipline that will clear off your schedule. It forces us to set aside time for intense pleading and listening to God. As we fast, you can search the Scriptures for His wisdom. I encourage you to invite trusted friends into the fast with you so they can support you in the desire of seeking God's plan for you on His mission.

After a season of fasting, you will have a sharper perspective of your own heart and the heart of God. Make no mistake, it will be difficult. Each time it will be difficult. But it will be worth it. The discipline will become a joyful departure from the normal pace of life as you engage God as your sole meal of grace.

Chapter 6

A PARTYING PEOPLE:

THE PRACTICE OF FELLOWSHIP

I did not build many things as a kid. Whatever natural creativity needed to spontaneously come up with fortresses, creatures, and vehicles simply did not exist in my brain.

However, one Christmas Day my parents gave me a giant set of Legos, complete with a large police station and one police helicopter. For hours I sorted through the blocks. Carefully following the instruction manual, I set every piece in place. Slowly, the walls came into shape at different locations around the set. Then the roof was put in place. Vehicles were built and little Lego people were arranged in their spots.

Finally, it was done. My bedroom was safe from evildoers because the Lego police patrol was on the scene. Everything was in its place.

During the construction, I just knew that this 4 by 4 piece fit onto that 6 by 6 piece at such-and-such angle because the instructions said so. Placing little pegs into smallish indentations made the blocks hold together. Looking back, I now realize the importance of all of the pegs and indentations. Without them, the building blocks would have just teetered precariously upon one another. The slightest bump would have caused everything to fall apart. But Legos have something special: an interlocking mechanism. It is simple. But it works.

The same is true of a practice that few of us ever think of as a spiritual discipline: fellowship. This discipline reflects a deep truth and requires a significant amount of effort . . . if you do it properly. Clearly it is one of the disciplines that cannot be accomplished in solitude. You must be with other believers to pull it off.

But there is something that must also happen in the privacy of your heart for it to be effective.

THE LONELIEST CROWD

Americans in the cities and suburbs often live in crowded places. The next time you're at a train stop or in the grocery store, just look around at all of the miserable faces. Sure, they might be that way because they'd rather be home, at the park, or just about anywhere else. But take a moment to see how disconnected they all are. In an age of smartphones, instant information, and social media that should keep us more connected than ever, we are just a lonely crowd of people. I pass through airports frequently and it is amazing to see how no one looks at each other. We live in a looking-down society.

Every now and again, something happens that reconnects us for a few moments. It can take on the form of something serious such as a national tragedy like the 2013 Boston Marathon bombing or something lighthearted like the feel-good

Disney movie *Frozen*. On the one end, we all grieve with one heart. On the other end, we all sing with one voice. "Let it go. Let it go. I'm one with the wind and something, something, something . . ." Admit it—you know the words.

Our Social and Spiritual Disconnections

Our social disconnection reveals our spiritual disconnection. Without a transformative experience, we will always be alone. Even in a crowded room, our disconnection from each other is not just because we lack shared interests. We cannot deeply connect without our sinful hearts being redeemed by Jesus. Once transformed by Him, then we must regularly maintain our relationship with Him. As our relationship with Christ is kept clear of sinful obstacles, only then can we truly enjoy the spiritual discipline of fellowship with one another.

Can we befriend one another without the power of Christ at work within us? Sure. Plenty of lost people and apathetic Christians enjoy deep friendships. But there is a completely different level of spiritual fellowship that we can obtain when the gospel is at the center of it all. As believers, we have the greatest answer to the lonely nature of human existence. Rather than scrap and claw for survival of the fittest, we have a community that highlights redemption. The communal life of the church reflects the love of God shown to man. As His people, we do not just display God intellectually or theologically. We show off His attributes in the way we live.

Loving Others Requires a Discipline of the Soul

When Jesus was asked about the greatest commandment in the Law, His answer was quick and clear. Love God with every part of your being and the second is like it, love your neighbor as yourself (Matt. 22:36–39). Love is never optional.

But remember, love requires discipline of the soul. It is not natural. Selfishness is natural to us. Love appears regularly for us only when we make it a habit. With fellowship, we find something that is occurring at a surface level constantly for the church. But I want to invite you to push further into fellowship as a community-born discipline that aids in propelling the mission of God.

A TOGETHER FAITH

The journey of faith is best taken with friends, both old and new. As believers, we need to embrace this idea. Our culture tells us to forge our own path and "pull yourself up by your own bootstraps" (though I'm not sure what a bootstrap actually is). The Bible paints a different picture.

In his letter to the Ephesian church, Paul wrote:

> Then we will no longer be little children, tossed by the waves and blown around by every wind of teaching, by human cunning with cleverness in the techniques of deceit. But speaking the truth in love, let us grow in every way into Him who is the head—Christ. From Him the whole body, fitted and knit together by every supporting ligament, promotes the growth of the body for building up itself in love by the proper working of each individual part. (4:14–16)

The passage highlights some important features about how fellowship helps to form us as believers. We are not called to simply walk alone in the life of faith. The very basis of Christianity is relationship. Through the person and work of Christ, we have a redeemed relationship with God. By His work in us, Christ connects us to His redeemed people to bear His reputation and carry out His mission. It is a life that requires more than just proximity to one another. A life that is set apart for Christ is one that not only communes with others but enjoys it.

The Greek term used in the New Testament that we translate as "church" is *ekklesia*. In its basic form, it means "the called-out ones." We are not just a random group of people who show up at the same place to sing the same songs and study from the same holy book. Rather, we are collectively called out by God to accomplish His work according to His gospel.

"Fitted Together"

Paul addressed foundational ideas for this discipline to the Ephesians. He shows us the need for fellowship to be authentic. Using the phrase "fitted and knit together" does not allow for surface-tension relationships. "Surface tension" is the scientific name for the phenomenon when the surface of the water does not break but holds in place; like when a small water bug skims across it or a drop of water lands on your fingertip. The surface seems solid but actually takes very little pressure for the molecules to break from one another. We can do better. We must.

We hold on to a personal faith but not a private faith. To the church in Rome, Paul wrote, "We who are many are one body in Christ and individually members of one another" (Rom. 12:5). We have a together faith. Engaging fellowship as a community means moving through our messy interdependence. We are not just coexisting as believers. We work at a life joined together for the working out of our faith. It can be messy. Our faith does not allow for just casual acquaintances. We are partners in one another's growth and God's passion to see restoration take place throughout the world.

A Loving Spirituality

Fellowship is also a loving spirituality. Paul had to remind the Ephesians that we are to speak the truth in love (4:15). It requires the truth of the Scriptures as a whole and the gospel in particular. Because we often falter at applying these to ourselves, we need the church, our small group, and our Christian friends to do so for us. But we are not seeking to grow just for the sake of becoming a huge religious organization. We want growth because we already have love. Being built on the character of God's love, we desire the best for one another.

As a father, you would expect for me to say that I love my sons. As I write this, Andrew is a sophomore in college and Chris is a senior in high school. Sometimes they drive me crazy. On the other hand, I drive them crazy all of the time. But we love each other. We want to help each other grow as men. It's my job, my duty, my honor, and my joy to help them grow. But growth is more than just an intellectual enterprise. It is more than mere moralism. I want to help them love Christ as deeply as possible. To do so, we have to allow one another deeply into our lives. When fellowship is engaged as a spiritual discipline, then we can allow such relationships to take place.

Fellowship as a spiritual discipline also means that we engage in joint ministry. Paul taught the Ephesians that "the whole body . . . promotes the growth of the body for building up itself in love by the proper working of each individual part" (v. 16). Ministry is not an individual endeavor. When we habitually seek holiness, we do it together. God's intention is to multiply believers so that we can be joined together to Him and to one another. We are knit together with the love of God so that we can build up the body.

FELLOWSHIP THAT BRINGS GROWTH

The habit of fellowship should result in growth. The growth we seek is twofold. We want to mature as believers and we want to multiply our numbers. Neither should happen at the expense of the other.

In John 15, Jesus described Himself as the vine and His believers as branches. The work that He will do through us will produce fruit. Jesus described our relationship to the fruit in three ways. He says that we will produce fruit (v. 2). Then He says we will produce "much fruit" (v. 5). Then He adds that we will produce fruit that will remain (v. 16). All of this productivity is set in the context of our fellowship with Christ and love for one another. These are intrinsically linked ideas in the mind of God. It plays out in the passage through Christ's description of us.

When we come to faith in Christ, we are confessing that He is the rightful King over us. With all His authority, Jesus has the right to treat us however He chooses. If honest, given that kind of power we would lord it over one another. Once again, God shows us a better way. In the John 15 passage, Jesus says, "I do not call you slaves anymore, because a slave doesn't know what his master is doing. I have called you friends, because I have made known to you everything I have heard from My Father" (v. 15). The implications are staggering. In His final week before the crucifixion, Jesus is instructing the disciples who consistently failed to understand His teachings. He can lead them toward anything: end-of-the-world theology, how to be master teachers, fundraising, or international mission work. He can deem them anything: followers, students, children, or servants. But He chooses the role of friend.

It takes discipline to relate to others in this way. Friendship comes easily enough. Common interests or stage of life can create friendships. Working together or many years as neighbors can do it too. But spiritual friendship takes a discipline that moves beyond proximity to one another during hobbies. Desiring the spiritual growth and mutual participation in God's mission is where mere friendship becomes the spiritual discipline of fellowship.

THE WORK OF A BODY

A Spiritual Friendship

The discipline of fellowship is worked out in numerous ways, beginning with that level of spiritual friendship among us. The Christian classic *Experiencing God*, by Henry Blackaby, has been translated into dozens of languages. To many, Blackaby is a spiritual giant. Some years ago, I served as an associate pastor in the church where he and his wife are members. During my tenure, Henry was gracious to meet me for a meal periodically for us to talk about faith, family, and life in general.

At the end of one particular breakfast, I went into a sappy rant about how grateful I was to have Henry in my life, that he would share his wisdom with me, and that no one could ever ask for a better mentor. Then, he looked at me so strangely and said words that I will never forget. "Philip, I'm just your friend." I learned more in those five words than I've likely taught in a hundred sermons.

Henry had every human reason to lord over me, call me his student, and remind me of his many years of following the Master. But those thoughts never crossed his mind. He simply considered us to be two men traveling together on the same road of faith in Jesus. He understood the friendship afforded to him by Christ and enjoyed the opportunity to share it with another.

Fellowship as friendship moves like a ripple in a lake. There is no need for us to make large, cannonball splashes with one another. The arrogance of letting everyone know you showed up is counter to the spiritual fellowship that focuses on the good of others. Fellowship is often a quiet discipline that began on one side of the church and has made its way to us. The work that was done in Henry's life impacted me at a breakfast more than ten years ago. His humble friendship causes me to carefully navigate my relationships as a husband, father, and

> *Henry's humble friendship causes me to carefully navigate my relationships as a husband, father, and church member.*

church member. In some arenas of life, I have plenty of authority but I've learned that I'd rather have friendship.

Living out our faith together means loving one another

well. The love of Christ that we share manifests itself in ministering to a world that is desperate for authentic relationships. What affects us as believers in the church will impact us as witnesses in the world.

Being Conduits of His Grace

Over time, standing water, lacking movement, becomes stagnant, but flowing water stays fresh. Similarly, fellowship as a discipline has movement. In chapter 7 we will look at the discipline of rest because we all need it. Fellowship engages with spiritual discernment to help our friends recognize the difference between rest and laziness. When we allow the grace of God to flow into our lives without further release to those around us, it spoils the ultimate purpose. God's mission to make us holy includes each of us but does not end with any one of us.

As we engage fellowship as a discipline of mutual disciple-making and mission, God then uses us as conduits for displaying His glory. Our interactions become ripples of grace that touch one another's lives.

Protecting One Another

In fellowship, we also find ways to protect one another. It takes discipline because we have to be on the lookout and have concern for one another. Fellowship is about enjoying one another for the spiritual connection we have in Christ. It also extends to the loving care that we give away freely because of spiritual friendship. But, as with all the disciplines, fellowship involves truth, the gospel, and God's character at work within us.

The protection stemming from fellowship runs a spectrum for us. Jude wrote, "Have mercy on those who doubt; save others by snatching them from the fire; have mercy on others but with fear, hating even the garment defiled by the flesh" (vv. 22–23). Fellowship is not just having the spiritual gift of casserole-ing one another. It means that we show grace to our friends when they struggle. Looking out for the spiritual development of friends means patience through their times of learning, misunderstanding, and even doubting. It is why it requires effort. It's easier to turn up your nose and walk away from the doubter. But if we want to look like Jesus, we stay, as He did with the apostles.

Jude also teaches us to live out this discipline by protecting one another from temptation. We are the ones who reach into the fire to pull out our friend who is in danger. We don't turn a blind eye when the gospel is misapplied or goes unapplied in someone's heart. The glory of Christ alive in our friend's life means so much to us that we don't want them to miss it or to cast it aside. We intervene with the truth—which is what Jude's little letter is all about—with a violent grace to snatch someone from spiritual danger. We love the lost so much that we go on a rescue mission for them. We love the believer so much that we reapply the truth of Scripture to them. We love God so much that we want every friend to experience the full gamut of His work in them.

Fellowship runs along a wide spectrum of activity. In the church, it mirrors the kind of work that Jesus has accomplished for us. Personally, it is costly because you are setting self aside for the better result in someone else's life. Two key areas by which we benefit others as part of fellowship are hospitality and advancing God's mission.

FELLOWSHIP AND HOSPITALITY

One very natural and biblical expression of fellowship as a discipline toward mission is biblical hospitality. In fact, an entire book could be dedicated just to this subject, so I hope you will study it more fully on your own. But think quickly with me about it in light of these verses.

> You must regard the foreigner who lives with you as the native-born among you. You are to love him as yourself, for you were foreigners in the land of Egypt; I am Yahweh your God. (Lev. 19:34)
>
> Share with the saints in their needs; pursue hospitality. (Rom. 12:13)
>
> So then you are no longer foreigners and strangers, but fellow citizens with the saints, and members of God's household, built on the foundation of the apostles and prophets, with Christ Jesus Himself as the cornerstone. (Eph. 2:19–20)
>
> Be hospitable to one another without complaining. (1 Peter 4:9)

The Bible is a story of hospitality. God creates a home for Adam and Eve in Genesis. He has prepared a new home for us in Revelation. Everything between those bookends of the Bible consistently reveals God's heart for welcoming home the straggler, the stranger, and the struggler. Christian hospitality should do the same. When fellowship is fully engaged, we follow Paul's directive in Romans 12 to "pursue hospitality." Fellowship is hanging out casually, but that's not all it is. We must go after those who are lonely and without hope. Hospitality is done with the memory that we were once the stranger who was offered a dinner invitation.

Now that we are insiders, let's go get the outsiders. All around us, people are asking a simple question that scares them to answer honestly: "Do I fit in here?" By Christ's grace, the answer can be yes. Invite them into your life for friendship that goes beyond the surface conversations about the latest movie. Hospitality extends beyond eating and talking together to inviting others into your life.

Pride, busyness, selfishness, and fear—all these may keep us from showing hospitality. Instead we must see the exhausted single mother who needs a break, or the hurting teen who needs a listening ear. Seek out the immigrant needing a friend. Let the new family in the neighborhood know that they actually belong here. Take the widows and widowers in to your circle of friendship like they truly matter.

The antidote to all of our selfish sins of hiding from the world is to imitate the radical generosity of Jesus. Fellowship becomes a missional discipline when we allow hospitality to welcome the stranger into our lives so they can see a reflection of grace alive in us.

THE MISSION OF FELLOWSHIP

Beyond hospitality, there are other ways that fellowship sets us out on God's mission. We often think of missionary endeavors and church planting being accomplished by individuals, yet in the New Testament accounts such activities were mainly done by groups of believers. There are, of course, places in the Bible where individuals were faithful without the help of others. But as we've seen and as you read the Scriptures, it is God's intention that His mission be carried out by His people collectively. Israel was set aside to be a nation that displayed God's glory. The church is a people who together reflect the good news of Christ. We work in a plurality to see God's message of salvation invade our community and the ends of the earth. We partner with one another for the gospel mission.

Ephesians 3:10 says, "God's multi-faceted wisdom may now be made known through the church to the rulers and authorities in the heavens." You as an individual can rely on the whole church to be a change agent to the highest power in culture and government. When we consider the injustices, inequities, and social ills tolerated by the leaders of countries, no believer is standing alone when he stands up for the gospel. As we carry the message of justice, we do so together because God chose to make His wisdom known not through Lone Ranger Christians but through the church. As the "called out ones," we do this together.

IMMORTALS AMONG US

One final thought that is part encouragement and part caution. Our mission is always relational, so never use people for evangelistic target practice and illustrations of social do-gooding. Drive-by ministry devalues the lost and is insulting to the Christ who died for the sake of redeeming broken people.

People are too important to simply use as playthings to bolster our egos. The gospel is too important to not handle with more care.

C. S. Lewis once wrote,

> All day long we are, in some degree, helping each other to one or other of these destinations. It is in the light of these overwhelming possibilities, it is with the awe and the circumspection proper to them, that we should conduct all of our dealings with one another, all friendships, all loves, all play, all politics. There are no *ordinary* people. You have never talked to a mere mortal. Nations, cultures, arts, civilisations—these are mortal, and their life is to ours as the life of a gnat. But it is immortals whom we joke with, work with, marry, snub, and exploit—immortal horrors or everlasting splendors.[1]

It makes me pause to think about how I consider the people around me. If we find that people are treated as interruptions, then we've got it wrong. The love that we have for God must manifest itself in a love for those He sends across our paths.

After all, you've never accidentally met anyone. Instead, God—being God—organizes your life so that you can have an effect on every person you meet. We foolishly think the choice to interact or ignore is a function of time and personal convenience. It is not. The person before you for a moment or for good is a mission-shaped opportunity. We should welcome them as the image-bearer for God that they are; with a disposition of joy and an urgency to see God's image unmarred by Christ's grace exclaimed to them by our lips and lives.

We have the moments of light and love not just to share with Christ alone. We share them with one another. The immortals around us all have a destiny. The fellowship of the saints increases our joy and pleases our Father. The hospitality shown toward all men and women swings wide the gate of grace for the non-Christian to see grace, to understand love, and to respond to the gospel.

Chapter 7

DRIVING IN
THE SLOW LANE:

THE PRACTICE OF REST

Living in the suburbs, I get up and face the task of driving downtown each day of the workweek. Over the last few years, in an attempt to get ahead of traffic, I've awoken earlier and earlier. And earlier. But it's been no help, because apparently everyone else in my city has done the same thing.

We all are leaving for work earlier than before in order to beat the traffic jam that we're creating by all getting an earlier start. It is maddening.

But I found a solution. It is one that I don't really like but it works: driving in the slow lane. Yes. I know. It sounds ridiculous. After the many attempts to rush to work and the other days spent just puttering along in the right lane, I've discovered a truth. I'm not saving any significant time by weaving in and out of traffic at breakneck speed. For every person I cut off in traffic, another person cuts me off. So, I stay in the slow lane and take my sweet time getting to the office.

Surely you don't believe that last sentence. Good, because I'm like most of my road-warrior competitors, fighting and clawing for every inch of traffic space. Why? Because my brain tells me that by going fast and being busy, I win. But when I'm so busy with the go, go, go attitude, I usually need a metaphorical crash. (Not a real one. That would be bad.)

HURRY SICKNESS

Many of us suffer from the malady of hurry sickness. We will buy into anything that will help us save time. It is why companies like Domino's Pizza are so successful. They are not selling just pizza and sandwiches. They are selling the convenience of delivery. In other words, they appear to sell you the one commodity you cannot get no matter how hard you try: time.

Other places do it as well, of course. That's why we have drive-through lanes at fast-food restaurants, call-ahead ordering—even at some sit-down restaurants—and mobile apps that give us the perfect route whether we travel by train, car, or foot.

The hurry that we inflict upon ourselves is not from a chaotic schedule. Hurry is a sign of a chaotic heart. For all the effort we place into saving ourselves a bit of time, we have actually lost the sense of timelessness. Shortsightedness has robbed us of living well. We never seem to have enough time. Consequently, we lose sight of eternity.

Think with me about the symptoms of our hurry sickness. For one, you and I are always looking for the fastest lane. From the red lights to checkout lines, algorithms float through our minds to determine which will shave seventeen seconds from the task at hand. Then comes the multitasking. Time management experts repeatedly tell us that multitasking does not really save you any time on a given task. But we like the feeling of progress on multiple fronts, so we give in to the deception. It can be seen in workspaces and homes either being utterly cluttered or immaculately clean. The extremes show a complete abandonment because someone spends no time in cleaning—or an obsessive expenditure of time thinking that somehow tidiness will make life seem more orderly.

The hurry sickness then shows up in our relationships. We find either tolerance or actual enjoyment in having superficial relationships. Not wanting to invest time in the hard work of people, we find solace in the "How are you?" and "Just fine" conversations of life. Hurry sickness manifests itself to the people we care most deeply about as what others refer to as "sunset fatigue." It is that feeling that you've given every ounce of strength to completing tasks and have nothing left for the members of your family.

We find ourselves losing the very ability to care. It is detrimental to our relationships at home, in the community, and in the church. Hurry and love fundamentally reach incompatible levels.

GOD'S EXAMPLE OF REST

The hurry sickness obviously has more than just an earth-bound effect. From the beginning, God had the intention that we would take a different pace with life. In the creation week, He gave us a rich example, and a rich reward. God set aside working on the seventh day to create the Sabbath. It was completely unnecessary for God to take a momentary break. He is God. By His very nature of omnipotence, He does not need to rest. Instead, the Lord takes an entire day to cease His work in order to show us how to live better. Now, you and I find ourselves in need of disciplining ourselves to live as God intended.

If we ignore this set of disciplines, we will, in fact, ignore God and His work in our lives. It sounds alarming on purpose. The go-go-go and do-do-do attitude by Christians is often born from the idea that God has secured our eternal destiny but I need to work hard to make Him love me. In that, we are completely wrong. Refusing to rest in the work of Christ, we try our level best to add to our own reputation before God. The more we strive to prove ourselves worthy, we accomplish the opposite. It becomes a vicious cycle of working harder to satisfy God's justice and thereby proving how much our sin actually deserves.

WHAT ARE WE BEING ASKED (NOT) TO DO?

Resting in Our Relationships

The spiritual disciplines in this arena go by different names, yet all are shades of the same color. In general, we are looking at the discipline of rest. But we can also see it as slowing, solitude, retreat, and even silence. Now, before you drop this book in fear that the following sections are going to send you to a monastery, keep calm and read on. With such disciplines, God is not calling you to a life of loneliness but to one of focus. It might entail times of focused separation. But the gospel is built on relationship, and God is not doing anything to undermine this approach for us.

Resting to Rely on God

As is true with all of the disciplines, the practice of rest is intended to keep us from a mediocre expression of faith. When we rest, we show our need for God's presence to sustain and fulfill us. Rest removes the self-reliant attitude that joy comes through personal attainment. It is in this place that we can begin to understand what God intended for believers with the Sabbath rest. We don't slow down just for the sake of sanity but also for sanctification.

In its most basic form, the Sabbath is the day set aside for rest and reflection. In ancient times, observing this practice was also a sign of faith. For the mostly agrarian nature of life, tending to the crops and the livestock was a necessity for staying alive. Ceasing one's labor for the Sabbath was a practice of faith that God is the true Provider. The New Testament church instituted worship to occur on the Sabbath (Sunday) because it is the day that Christ rose from the dead. The Sabbath took on the meaning for us that the spiritual work for our salvation had been attained by Jesus.

> *We don't slow down just for the sake of sanity but also for sanctification.*

We do not need to strive, scratch, or claw toward God's approval by keeping the Law. We rest in knowing that Christ's labor for our salvation was, is, and will always be enough.

Later in the New Testament, in the book of Hebrews, the

Sabbath receives an even deeper meaning for us. We learn that the earthly Sabbath rest of one day a week represents an eternal reality. While we rest for this single day, it points us toward the rest that we will receive for all days. The eternal reward we inherit in our salvation is the rest that always satisfies.

But in the meantime, we must remember the transitory nature of the Sabbath practice. It was Jesus Himself who reminded the legalists, "The Sabbath was made for man and not man for the Sabbath." Our Lord wants us to see that this discipline is made for our own good. It is a natural connection built into life's schedule to show our affection for God and love Him for His provisions. Like all disciplines, it is not to be used as a fulcrum to leverage God into owing us anything. He uses it in our lives to remind us of everything we have inherited.

If hurry is a disease, we need not look far for a cure. In fact, the first few chapters of this book serve as the foundation for this discipline as they do for others. I want to give you a few facets to this discipline that should help us understand it better. But all along the way, keep the ideas of worship, Bible engagement, and prayer at the forefront of your mind.

Resting Our Bodies

There is something to be said for a good nap. Babies like them. Teenagers need them. But then something happens to adults. We avoid them like they will ruin our productivity. Perhaps that is exactly what we need *for* productivity.

On the first Sabbath, God rested. The Hebrew term for Sabbath means to cease exertion. There is not a hidden idea to the original term. It just means to stop working. When we stop trying so hard, it is a time when we give the Holy Spirit a place to speak clearly through the Word. It also has a serious theological implication for us. As a believer, you have trusted Christ for your salvation. But too many of us deem it necessary to work like madmen in a bid to keep God happy with our level of morality and do-gooding. Resting is the reminder that He does not need your morality or social activity to preserve your salvation.

Resting does not take any effort. If it does, then you're doing it wrong. But it does take a level of discipline for most of us. In 2011, at the age of forty-one, my left carotid artery spontaneously collapsed and I suffered a mini-stroke. A neurologist stood by my hospital bed and actually said these sentences: "You really dodged a bullet. Most people die." My doctors told me to take several weeks off work and rest. I suddenly learned how bad I was at resting. My body, emotions, and soul needed the rest. But my production proclivities kept my mind racing.

By the end of several weeks, I had learned an important lesson about why rest matters. The resting helped me to look around. My appreciation for my wife, my kids, and just life in general all increased. As I rested, the Lord worked over my heart and gave me time for evaluations, repentance, and restoration. I wish it had not taken a serious health crisis to learn it all.

Here is a helpful reminder: God accepted you into His family because of Jesus' work, not yours. So take a break. Give yourself a break. Rather than fret about the thing you must do next—even if it is a good thing—enjoy a Sabbath break.

Slowing the Pace

Resting means that you stop altogether. But I think part of the discipline is also found in simply slowing down. Remember the idea of driving in the slow lane. There is a freedom in knowing that you do not have to be in a hurry.

As a kid, I camped quite a bit. Growing up in the suburbs, I learned to appreciate the forest. As an adult, there is one aspect of being on a trail, in a park, or in the woods that holds out a great gift for me. It is the opportunity to walk slowly. When my sweet wife, Angie, can prevail upon me to stop working and go out for a break, it becomes a beautiful moment because of what it does for my soul. The physical discipline to slow down my steps—and the rest of my life—usually translates to stilling my heart before Jesus.

Slowing down is not a major act of faith for some people. But for those of us whose self-image is deeply wrapped up in how much we produce, slowing down is good for us. In it, we can set aside the crashing pace of work and the crushing pressure to perform. When you slow down, take up the Scriptures and allow them to set your pace.

Solitude and Retreats

The majority of the world's population lives in urban and suburban areas, constantly surrounded by other people. It begs the question as to when we can simply be alone with God. At what point can you spend extended time with God and His Word in order to grow in your faith?

Hopefully, you are spending time on a daily basis in God's Word and in prayer. Many of the disciplines—even some parts of rest—can be practiced as a normal part of life's pace. But looking at Jesus, we see that He broke away from life's pace on several occasions. In the Gospels, we see Jesus remove Himself not just from the crowds but also from the apostles. He would go to a solitary place in order to more deeply commune with the Father. If Jesus chose to do so, think of how much more we need it. Christ began His ministry with forty days of fasting and solitude in the wilderness (Matt. 4:1–11). Before He chose the twelve men to serve as His apostles, He spent a night alone (Luke 6:12). Even in a time of mourning, we see Jesus retreat into solitude upon hearing about the death of John the Baptist (Matt. 14:13).

The retreats were used by Jesus to spend focused time with the Father. While living in perfection, He did not need to repent or change His mind over anything. It was, instead, time spent in relational closeness with the Father. It afforded Jesus time to live separately from the distractions of normal life.

Henri Nouwen has called solitude "the furnace of transformation."[1] It is a time in which God can burn off the extraneous from our lives. Solitude is the place where we can gain momentary freedom from the forces of culture. Rather than fight, it is the proper time to flee. Only, in this instance we don't flee in fear but with joy to things of value, things that last.

Growing up in church, the teens in our youth group would go on both a summer and winter retreat. In the summer we went to Panama City Beach, Florida, and in the winter we went to Gatlinburg, Tennessee. They are both fine cities but neither really offers a retreat from the world. In fact, for a teenage boy, the beach

> *Solitude is "the furnace of transformation," a time in which God can burn the extraneous from our lives.*

normally offered more distractions rather than less. In Gatlinburg, we were surrounded by the whirring, flashing, nonstop buzz of go-cart tracks, souvenir shops, and candy stores. Just the memories make me a little tired. It was often the opposite of a "retreat." The fundamental need we have is separation. We need to disconnect from the attention-grabbing world that we live in each day.

Whether for an hour or a week, the opportunity to be away from the world's barrage of influence is good for our spiritual formation. Without those distractions, I can more easily give my heart's affection to Christ. The breaks in the rapid pace of life (or rabid craving for my attention) set me up for a more regular attentiveness to Jesus.

Silence

As I write this paragraph, my younger son Chris is in the next room playing a basketball video game. My wife is downstairs singing. My older son Andrew just blew through my room to make noise; because he is a teenager, he does that. A final facet to rest is silence—and it is hard to come by. To be honest, finding a place of silence in my life normally requires one particular thing: the absence of all other people. But it is actually a much more nuanced experience.

"Be still, and know that I am God," Psalm 46:10 (NIV) tells us. We need to find ways to heed this verse. Stillness is often an odd occurrence in our schedules. In my life, it requires a literal silence. To achieve it, I must still myself and my world. It is a toss-up determining the more difficult of the two. But rest requires quiet. So as you engage in times of rest, don't just substitute running around for sitting still among distracting surroundings. Instead, be quiet before God. This is much like fasting. Remember that fasting without prayer is just a bad diet. Silence and rest without focusing on God is just a brief break from your chores. We want to be quiet so that God can have the place to speak to us.

As you seek a literal silence, it may mean a silence of your workweek. The kind of quiet you regularly need means a separation from the noise of your daily responsibilities. Finding a way to have "work silence" takes a bit of faith. It is not about missing work for a day as much as it is about not allowing work to rule your day. The believer should trust Christ deeply enough to know that work will be there in the morning or whenever one returns. The silence of our stilled work is a time to better focus on the gospel's active work in us.

> *It is not about missing work for a day as much as it is about not allowing work to rule your day.*

One other facet we need for rest is "digital silence." Currently, I am within thirty feet of the following: a television, three video game consoles, a Blu-ray player, two laptops, e-reader, home telephone, and my smartphone. At any given moment, we have access to the sum total of human knowledge contained on the Internet and more entertainment media than we could consume in a few lifetimes. Rest and silence need their complete attention. I suggest that you turn off and away from the devices that scream for your attention. Quite literally they call to us with notifications that never stop from email, apps, and social media. As you engage in this discipline, do so in such a way that God has your undivided attention.

OXYMORONIC RESTING

How do we rest *together*? After all, you have just read two-thirds of a chapter that advocates the need to be alone. Still, as we've seen with the previous disciplines, rest also needs to be practiced with a group. Extroverts typically can do it easily. If you are an introvert reading this book you probably just saw your life flash before your eyes. Resting—with people around?! That seems an impossible oxymoron.

Let me suggest three different ways that you can practice rest in all of its forms with other believers.

Retreats with Others

The first is likely the most obvious: taking retreats together. For too many of us, retreats are relegated as only for the children's and student outings. But consider the powerful nature of rest when adults in a Bible study group, a collegiate group, or even an entire church decides to retreat from the world's influence for a little while. In such a time, we can fight off the muck that our lives have been swamped by and find clarity in our decision-making. It is a time when accountability becomes more natural to our relationships because of the intentionality of spending time with one another. Changing our location to a place that is remote, or just different, can help us gain perspective. Rest can be solitude but does not necessitate it. In my own life, I need other believers to take me aside and help me lie low for a while. It can be a time for board games, hiking, or whatever allows you to recharge in the company of friends.

As we practice this together, it does not have to be formal but it should not be haphazard. I've taken retreats where the agenda was to pray, discuss the Scriptures, and pray some more. There were no games of Ping-Pong, hanging out on a beach, or other fun-for-fun's-sake activities. Sometimes it is exactly what your friends need. But it is not a place to be legalistic. Disciplines are inherently for the display of love toward God and how it spills over to others. Choosing a location and the right activity/inactivity helps us to do it with intentionality. No matter what, we need to focus our lives together on God's agenda for our holiness and His mission. But do not be a slave to a practice. Remember, the Sabbath was made for you. Your group of friends was not made to fulfill the Sabbath.

Simply Relaxing with Church Friends

The pace of the church is another place where we can work together in the community discipline of rest. I've served as a pastor of one sort or another for most of my adult life. We are often the guilty parties for planning activities at such a pace that no one can get any rest. The hours not spent at work and for chores are suddenly all given over to the various programs placed on the church calendar. All in all, they are good things to do. But when you feel yourself run ragged by religious responsibilities, the temptation is to fall prey to legalism. We need to ensure that the pace of ministry at the church has the urgency involved with evangelizing the world while also caring for believers' souls.

My encouragement to church members in general and church leaders in particular is that we not take up the mantle of the Pharisees. Busying ourselves before one another, the world, and especially God is simply not impressive. Everybody is busy. If you sacrifice people's souls on the altar of religious activity, then we've destroyed the display of the gospel. Tell people to go home to their families and to hang out with their friends armed with the ability to promote love and good deeds among them. Let them rest in the grace that the church rightly proclaims.

In the prior chapter, we looked at fellowship as a spiritual discipline. Simply enjoying time with each other with no agendas and strings attached is a third way we can rest together.

We can rest in many ways. Let's give game nights, cookouts, and days at the lake sitting in hammocks the spiritual significance they deserve. Rather than needing something from one another, we simply need each other's presence. In so doing, we can also listen closely to one another for the Spirit's movements in their lives. As we rest together, engage your faith to discuss God's provisions so that it becomes more than a day off.

THE MISSION OF RESTING

Resting does not sound very missional until you consider the hurried pace of our world. Then being the person at work or in the neighborhood who intentionally slows down life's pace takes on new meaning. Unbelievers are hustling every day to find meaning for their lives. Many seek power, accomplishments, and pleasure to feel worth in this world. All of those things take hard work. When believers rest, it makes us seem out of place—because we are.

Our lives can become different from the spiritually lost

when we slow our pace and become secure in Christ. When a lost person finds their worth in accomplishments and seeking out pleasure, they cannot rest. If they see us at rest, we may have an opportunity to talk about the gospel's power to give security. We rest to connect more deeply with God and show trust in Christ's provisions. Often the lost are busy with religious checklists hoping they can please a capricious god somewhere in the universe. (Or they are simply trying to please a capricious person on the earth.)

Our rest is a witness to our security found in Christ's provision through His resurrection. Rest is a testimony of deliverance from self-reliance. The difference in your self-image as a believer and theirs becomes apparent.

When you rest, people will want what you have. They just don't know that what you have is a relationship with God through faith. For us to take a day off for a Sabbath is an act of faith and a symbol of something more. Our earthly resting reflects our eternal rest. We are seeking an increased sensitivity to the voice of God. Being freed from dependence on human approval, we enjoy God's guarantee of abundant life here and eternal life to come.

As you rest, invite unbelievers to slow down with you. They have no idea what it means to truly trust God to be all they need. In their quest to achieve more and experience more, they are missing the One who can satisfy their souls. As you invite the lost into your rest, solitude, and even silent moments, do so because of the gospel. Let them clearly know that you silence yourself and slow down your life for the purpose of love. You know that God loves you deeply and you intend to hear from Him.

Chapter 8

POSSESSING POSSESSIONS:

THE PRACTICE OF SIMPLE LIVING

B ut what do you really want?

As a father, I've asked that question approximately 7,382,519 times over the last nineteen years. When my boys were very young, it was often a parental defense mechanism. "What do you want?!?" was synonymous for "If you'll stop crying, I'll buy any toy, give you any food, or sing any song your little heart desires." Now my sons are older. As their dad, I think they are the best young men on the planet. But they are teenagers, which means understanding what they would like for birthdays and Christmas is like deciphering a foreign language of grunts and shrugs.

Understanding what someone else wants is not easy. We peer into their lives hoping to find a clue. But we end up back in the same aisle at the superstore, picking through the same stuff as last year. The journey is repeated for each holiday and birthday.

Purchasing a gift for someone is tricky for a number of reasons. It is a game of discovering what will make them happy. It is why we need to deal with the issue of the source for joy. Our trouble is that our possessions often end up possessing us. We allow the things we own to become the driving force for us. If you think this is not true, then just consider the trajectory of our shopping.

As I write this, a grocery store chain currently uses this tagline in many of its commercials: "Where shopping is a pleasure." The idea is clear. Most people endure the chore of grocery shopping. This chain of stores wants us to enjoy it.

Now, grocery shopping is a necessity. We need food to survive and unless you live on a farm, the weekly trip to the grocery story is necessary. But there is an underlying premise to the tagline that is unhelpful. It is the idea that shopping brings happiness. Putting our hope in food or possessions leads us to a hopelessness that no earthbound thing can solve.

THE FALSE GOD OF MORE

In ancient times, the Hebrews faced a new adversary. When they moved into the Promised Land of Canaan, they discovered that the indigenous people worshiped the false god Baal. It was one of the primary gods in their religious system and was associated with agricultural success. The Canaanites sacrificed to Baal in the hopes for increase not just in their crops but also among their livestock and children in their own families. Additionally, many of the places dedicated to Baal worship included chambers for temple prostitutes (males) and sacred harlots (females). People engaged in all sorts of worship, sacrifices, and (ahem) other behaviors to gain Baal's blessings for more stuff in their lives.[1]

In a practical sense, Baal was the god of excess. He was the god of more. Sadly, the Israelites fell to the sin of worshiping the false god Baal on several occasions during the Old Testament era. Not satisfied with the Lord's commands and provisions, they chased after Baal's blessings. They called on Baal to supply where they felt the true God had failed them.

We are no different. We want more. The world defines success as gaining power, amassing possessions, and stacking up achievements. In order to be happy, you need more. Ironically, in our bid to gain more possessions and control our lives, the roles reverse and we become a slave to what we own.

Yet we know there is an unhealthy tipping point. It is why we have garage sales, yard sales, and auctions. We get rid of the stuff that we once thought to be a necessity. Then we use the money to buy other things that are the new necessity. Plus, we shop at other yard sales in order to buy the stuff they no longer desire but for some reason we desire it now. Then there are the shows like *American Pickers*, where two guys travel the back roads of America looking for treasures to stock their antique shops. They find items ranging from car parts to toys. They negotiate prices on bicycles and gas pumps. The key is that the items are collectible. They take the old "junk" to their stores in hipster neighborhoods—where it is sold to high-end clientele for a markup as vintage decor for their suburban homes.

That may sound ridiculous until you recognize the next unhealthy step on the possession spectrum: the show titled

Hoarders. In this show, people call in psychological and psychiatric professionals to confront their family members. In an hour, you can watch the mental sickness of a person so obsessed with their possessions that they have literally refused to throw away anything, including garbage. It is a tragic display of human angst. The source of any comfort in their lives comes from sheer accumulation. In such instances, they are truly possessed by their possessions.

THE PROBLEM OF OUR HEARTS

The benign yard sale and the unhealthy hoarding are merely shadows of the spiritual sins that the discipline of simplicity can address. The Tenth Commandment is to not covet anything that is owned by your neighbor (Ex. 20:17). Jealousy is listed among sins like drunkenness and sexual immorality in Romans 13. Jesus addressed the subject in Luke 12:15 by saying, "Watch out and be on your guard against all greed because one's life is not in the abundance of his possessions." It all highlights that our hearts are seeking a priority in life. The world is happy to offer you any number of things that will supposedly satisfy. God knows that it will all fail.

God's commands reveal that envy, jealousy, and lust are all a form of having our allegiances torn away from Him. The cowboy philosopher Will Rogers has said, "Too many people spend money they earned . . . to buy things they don't want . . . to impress people that they don't like."[2] Meanwhile, God has accomplished the work that gives us what we need so that we can be in loving communion with Him. The command He gives is not to ignore the world or what it offers. The entire book of

Ecclesiastes is a study of how we are to enjoy the world but not place it on the throne of our hearts. Instead, we can rightly relate to the stuff of earth by seeking to know and please God. Otherwise, the lust of the flesh and the jealousy of our hearts will eventually subjugate our will to the possessions we own. We have created another god; it is the god of discontent.

The accumulation of more things in our lives reveals a lack of faith toward God. When we are unwilling to practice this discipline, we are making a dangerous declaration. It is the statement toward heaven, "God, You and what You provide are not enough." I doubt any of us would actually say those words to God. But is that not what we are communicating when we grab for the things of this world hoping to find some meaning and satisfaction? It is what those outside of the faith do. Having found their satisfaction in the things of earth, they have missed the superior joys of knowing the God of heaven. Our lives are to be wholly different.

EMBRACING SIMPLICITY

The discipline of simplicity can become a caricature in many of our minds—we envision an impoverished religious order of men or women living in a commune. Every day they wear the same plain clothes, eat the same plain food, and live in the same plain environment. It is a life that is separated from the comforts, conveniences, and innovations of the modern era. It is intentionally lackluster, and everyone scowls a lot— probably from hunger and boredom.

You can choose to live that way, but just remember that God never asked for such a life from us in the Scriptures. It is true that Jesus did tell one rich man to sell everything he had, give the money to the poor, and then follow after Him. Jesus also told us that we cannot serve both God and money (Matt. 6:24). It is simply not possible to have two masters on one throne. We also know that Jesus said, "For where your treasure is, there your heart will be also" (Luke 12:34). So what are we to do with Christ calling us to place lesser value on things and more value on heart?

We can derive pleasure in this life from the God we serve. In John 10:10, Jesus highlighted that God wants us to live life to the fullest. *The call of God is not to separate from the world but to know how to live in it.* Yet as we practice the discipline of simplicity, we can live as holy people in a world of excess. We love Him rather than abundance of things.

Contentment

The discipline of simplicity has contentment at its heart. It is not the mere abandonment of things but setting things in their proper order. Being content is a pure act of faith. It is a declaration to God that however He wishes to provide, we will take joy in Him. Rather than whining for more, we will celebrate in the level of abundance He gives. When we practice simplicity, we put the highest value on the God who is the Giver rather than focusing on the pleasure that we receive from His gifts. That does not mean we ignore the good things we experience in life, but rather, we downgrade their importance in comparison to the surpassing greatness of God, our Supplier and chief delight.

Hebrews 13:5–6 teaches, "Your life should be free from the love of money. Be satisfied with what you have, for He Himself has said, I will never leave you or forsake you. Therefore, we may boldly say: The Lord is my helper; I will not be afraid. What can man do to me?" The Bible calls believers to reject our love of possessions because our faith lies with God. If you put all of your hope in what you can amass, then you must constantly guard it. That requires defending your possessions and even multiplying them to gain more happiness. For some, that leads to obsessing over those possessions. In contrast, contentment lets faith take root, which can subdue our striving and exertion.

Contentment versus Craving

Contentment also helps us to reject anything that produces addictive behavior in us. I use the term "addictive" in a broad, sweeping way. Substance addictions to alcohol, prescription medicines, and illegal drugs should be easily understood as drawing our hearts away from God. An addiction is something that requires professional and intensive treatment. In its worst form, it overtakes a life. In milder forms, the stuff of earth sways our allegiance and clamors for our attention. We may crave a morning cup of coffee, seek the runner's high, or yearn for the upgraded smartphone. We are not happy with what we have because we are sure there is something better. In its wost forms our discontent is like a slap in the face of the One who provides for us.

Instead, with contentment we are choosing an allegiance. I state that having Christ is all I need. When you and I are content, waiting becomes easier, because pleasure is found in time with Jesus. The running to attain more is replaced with a subtle rest in the One who gives enough. It is what Paul meant when he wrote the book of Philippians while imprisoned. One of the well-known verses of the book is 4:13: "I can do all this through [Christ] who gives me strength" (NIV). It is quoted by everyone from athletes about to take the winning shot to college students taking final exams. Some Christians use the verse as a lucky rabbit's foot to convince themselves that Christ wants them to "have it all." But that is pretty much the opposite of what Paul meant.

The reason we know that is the context. Look at the verses around it:

> I am not saying this because I am in need, for I have learned to be content whatever the circumstances. I know what it is to be in need, and I know what it is to have plenty. I have learned the secret of being content in any and every situation, whether well fed or hungry, whether living in plenty or in want. I can do all this through him who gives me strength. Yet it was good of you to share in my troubles. (Phil. 4:11–14 NIV)

In the ancient prisons of the Roman Empire, captives had nothing unless friends brought them provisions. Guards did not provide blankets, clothes, or food. Yet Paul wrote that he had learned to live with what he did (and did not) have. In his stark prison cell, all the former Pharisee had was Jesus. He was content to live only by what God would provide. He did not need fame, fortune, and power. The gospel was enough for Paul.

Contentment in a Social Media World

Contentment does not come easily in a social media world. Every time a neighbor gets a promotion, buys a new car, or just goes out to a new restaurant, we know about it. It is put on display for us to see . . . and be envious of their good fortune. But a life of simplicity will discipline our heart so that we need not hunger for another person's success. We become content because we enjoy God's provisions.

Simplicity affects both your view of what you own and also what you might purchase. Conforming ourselves for a holy lifestyle requires a continual learning curve about who we are in Christ. In developing our relationship with Jesus, we are reminded we are children of the King, who supplies our every need. When His covenant with us defines our identity, we are being content in Him. As a result, we are able to purchase things for their usefulness rather than for the status they can bring us. No longer do we need an expensive sports car to impress friends with our seeming wealth. My reputation is not wrapped up in that set of clothes or buying a gourmet coffee blend. Instead, Christ defines me perfectly without the need of earthly trappings.

STEWARDSHIP

We have a loving and giving God. We should not be a sedentary and stingy people. We have finances, abilities, and time that are available for someone to use. We can use them for the good of God's kingdom. In Luke 12, Jesus told the story of the rich fool who obsessed over building larger barns for all he possessed. He had no idea that he would be required to stand before the judgment seat of God so soon. He had wasted his efforts on amassing possessions rather than relating to the King.

"Stewardship" is living out the knowledge that God owns

all things and has entrusted us as the managers of the finances and possessions in our care. It is managing our temporary possession of what God ultimately owns. The rich fool forgot the principle that what was in his hands was there only temporarily, as all things come from God. This is true of everything we hold. I have money in my bank account that will go to the electric company, grocery store, mortgage company, for college tuition, and twenty other bills. When my paycheck arrives, I get the money for a short period of time. Even my retirement fund will be depleted in one way or another. I'll either use it up or it will pass on to others at my death.

> *Everything is under God's sovereign ownership. I'm just managing it for a little while.*

Everything is under God's sovereign ownership and I'm just managing it for a little while. The things I hold were not mine, are not mine, and will not be mine. Viewing possessions in this way allows me to live with less because I know the God who supplies bread for the hungry, clothes to the impoverished, and hope to the sinner. God is the one who supplies not just my needs but others' needs through me as well.

Paul wrote in 2 Corinthians 9:8, "God is able to make every grace overflow to you, so that in every way, always having everything you need, you may excel in every good work." When we choose to manage resources rather than grab for them, God's grace becomes more evident to us. We adjust our vision to see how He works rather than straining to do our own work. Stewardship is more than just having a budget. Through it, we understand the reason for our expenses, savings, and giving. Simplicity reframes our desire to be for God and not things. Stewardship aids in setting aside our possessions for God's purposes instead of our own.

With stewardship comes a relational aspect as well. Your church is more than a place to observe Sunday services. We are not consumers in a religious supercenter or audience members at a show. Believers are contributors and participants. Church membership is a weighty covenant in which we have joined our minds, hearts, and resources together with fellow Christians for a great endeavor. Giving is not an imposition but a gift. It is a gift that frees us from self-reliance and strengthens our faith.

When I take 10 percent or some other percentage of my salary to give to my local church, it is an act of faith with a huge return on the investment. By placing that money into the life of my church's ministry, my return on investment is eternal. We mature in our faith, grow in grace, and defeat our ego. Stewardship, as it feeds simplicity, is the tangible act where we financially state our faith in God. But it takes effort. After all, the bills must be paid and the groceries must be bought.

It is not just a passing thought but is an intentional act of the will. With this act, we tell God that we love Him more than the livelihood He has provided. In giving, we participate in a mirror-like act as Christ gave to us for our salvation.

SHUNNING

One final way that simplicity allows us to relationally connect deeper with God is through shunning. *Shunning* is avoiding those objects, thoughts, and even places that remove us from God. When this is a habit, we dismiss those things that steal away our gaze from God. Good stewards of God's grace should shun anything that distracts from seeking the kingdom of God and His righteousness as their priority. All relationships are based on choices and priorities. Shunning what is worldly allows you relational space to cling to what is holy.

In the language of the King James Version, it is a way that we mortify "the flesh" (Rom. 8:13). In shunning, we are killing the deeds of the flesh that hunger for more stuff. We happily choose less of this world so that we can have more of our relationship with God. Our faith expands, our affection for Christ grows, and our intimacy with Him is strengthened.

SIMPLY TOGETHER

By its nature, simplicity seems to be a spiritual discipline that can only be practiced by individuals. Perhaps it could be practiced by a family. However, the discipline, when lived out together by believers, has powerful results. After all, even a church must work to not be possessed by its possessions. As congregations, we can use financial giving as a measure for how people are progressing in their faith. But it is only one of many ways. As you think about how to practice this with others, let's think of a few ways that it is expressed.

Relationships

First Corinthians 13:4 reminds us, "Love does not envy." To choose simplicity is choosing to place people above possessions. In order to do that, you must have people around you to invest into. Simplicity, contentment, and shunning as habits will change our view of those around us. Rather than first noticing her in an outfit you wish you had, you see how flattering it looks on her. Instead of frustration that he got the promotion, you celebrate the success of your friend. Jealousy drives a wedge between friends. Contentment draws us closer because we can celebrate what someone else has gained. Make it a habit to care about the person before you even notice his or her possessions.

In doing so with our earthly relationships, it creates a place for the Holy Spirit to make you more discerning about the needs of your friends. The sins of jealousy and envy place roadblocks in our relationship with God because they are tacit accusations that He is unjust. The habitual celebration of what God has given to others further separates us from affection to the world's trinkets and makes us holy lovers of Jesus.

Generosity

The church should be a living example of generosity. Earlier, we looked at Philippians 4 regarding Paul's view of contentment. One of the keys to it is found in verse 14, where the apostle wrote, "Still, you did well by sharing with me in my hardship." We enable simple living and contentment in others by providing for them in the hard spaces of life.

The early church understood this very well. Acts 2:44–45 describes the first believers in this way: "Now all the believers were together and held all things in common. They sold their possessions and property and distributed the proceeds to all, as anyone had a need." Consider the change it would make in your church if everyone imitated the first-century church. Rather than hoarding our own possessions, we could develop the habit of giving to everyone who is in need. Widows, single moms, and the families struggling to make ends meet could be encouraged in ways that are completely countercultural.

As a family of faith, we need to develop the habit of giving away things to one another. If your car is broke down, you can borrow mine. When someone's washing machine is on the fritz, pick up their laundry and do it for them. When a widow is living far from her children, invite her over to dinner . . . regularly. These activities are not convenient but love rarely is convenient. It is costly. You know, like the cross. Taking our eyes off of self-preservation allows us to move into other-provision mode.

Discipling

Choosing simplicity does not come naturally to us. It requires learning from a great example. Perhaps this is where we can draw together as believers under this discipline. We must lead out and follow in discipling one another toward contentment and simplicity. We need one another's help in learning to shun selfishness, jealousy, and the desire for more.

As parents, we must commit to leading our children to value Christ and people over the things of the world. As a parent, I need the rest of the church to help me with this discipline. For starters, I need accountability in my own life for when I'm getting envious of others. Also, my kids need to see a community of people who value relationships over things. They suffer under the same barrage of commercials adults do that overpromise and under-deliver. But they've had less time to learn how to navigate the temptations. The church can disciple our children to place their priorities on relationships.

Parents should see the church family as a partner in this

process, and vice versa. Bible studies for children that feature stories focused on relationships first and all of our stuff later can teach our children the value of personal relationships. Then, by involving children in the work of ministry in the church, we put their focus primarily on how we welcome one another. In addition, parents and/or relatives can disciple children with the Scriptures that focus on fixing relationships and living out our faith. As we guard children from a bland moralism of "do better and get more" religion, they can clearly see the church living joyfully as one family.

An Attitude of Thanksgiving

Consider the impact if worship services more regularly focused on the provisions of God rather than on the need for more. When you think about what your church prays for and how it prays, calls of need should not outpace declarations of thanksgiving. As I pointed out in chapter 4 on prayer, asking God to supply our needs is good, appropriate, and necessary. But the petitions we make should be balanced with the gratitude we express.

The church has been given spiritual abundance. Most of us live with more than enough stuff in our lives. Certainly in comparison to most of the world, we who have the disposable income to spend on a book are among the more fortunate humans.

The petitions we make should be balanced with the gratitude we express.

Focusing on thanksgiving stems the tide of jealousy among us. It is a practice that can happen in worship services, small group

Bible studies, or just around a dinner table filled with friends. Collective thanksgiving sparks individual thanksgiving, and vice versa.

THE SIMPLE MISSION

Living in simplicity will make you stand out from the cultural norm. Although contentment and generosity are seen as character virtues, those two qualities are rarely demonstrated. Allowing them to be regular occurrences in your life—and thus pursuing God over things—will become a visible witness of the gospel, one that can yield fruitful conversations about your faith.

Generosity is itself a form of missional living. Giving anything away runs counterintuitive to our cultural standards. Particularly in the West, we negotiate for more, buy more, and keep more. Yet those who abide by the ethic of God's kingdom don't just give away more, they actually pursue generosity as a lifestyle.

Make no mistake about it. If you live by the values of God's kingdom, you will be questioned. People will wonder if you're saving enough for retirement and all manner of other things you need. As you find ways to be generous to unbelievers, they might question your motives. Great! It is an open door to describe God's generosity in sending Christ for us.

Contentment is also the witness of Christ's work in us. Unbelievers will not understand why you have "settled" for an old car, or why you don't scramble to attain the latest device or smartphone to hit stores. They might think your simplicity and contentment are strange. As you explain that your self-image, self-worth, and self-esteem come from your relationship with Christ, they will want to know more. Perhaps it will take a bit of time as they'll want to watch your life play out. But the persistent witness of a person who is happy with what they currently have will demand an explanation. Once again, it is an open opportunity for believers to discuss how they find their worth in Christ rather than in their possessions.

Simplified living will change your conversations as well. While neighbors hold conversations over who got the newest gadget, you will stand out. Rather than talk about the things people own, you can focus on the people who own the things. When you cease dwelling on and wanting what others have, it changes how you speak about other people. Compassion and honor become habitual. Thankfulness for how God has supplied good gifts to us becomes a natural topic.

We can live actively with our possessions as well. Using our possessions for the good of others is an idea that dates back to Old Testament times. God told the Israelites during their exile in a foreign land to settle down, build houses, have families, and "seek the welfare of the city" (Jer. 29:7). When you use what you own to bless the city where you live, your possessions become tools rather than idols. Our money and possessions are tools to assist us as we participate in God's kingdom.

If we trust money to bring us peace, anxiety is the normal result. We put ourselves at the whim of the stock market or a cranky supervisor. But if we will use our money, possessions, and the like for God's kingdom, then peace is the result. As Jesus taught us, value the treasures of heaven and you'll never want for anything more.

Chapter 9

THE MINISTRY OF THE MUNDANE:

THE PRACTICE OF SERVANTHOOD

The kingdom of God has an upside-down way about it. To gain, you must give. To be free, you must become a slave. To be first, you must be last. To be strong, you must be weak. To live, you must die. To succeed in life, you must serve.

But we live in a dog-eat-dog world. We hoard, demand our rights, rush to the front of the line, impose our will, fight to survive, and force others to care for our needs. We figure, *If I don't look out for myself, who will?* That is why Jesus appeared so strange to everyone then—and now. The miracle-working man from Nazareth never made demands that benefited Him. Instead, Jesus traveled around healing the sick, socializing with the outcast, and caring for everyone else. Whatever His needs were, people rarely heard about them.

The Jesus way of life remains one of servanthood. There

was simply never a sacrifice that seemed too great for Jesus to make. And that is His call to us: If you want to be first in God's kingdom, you must be a servant (Matt. 20:26).

On most days, I am not much like Jesus. Regularly, I want my waitress to move faster. I want my coworkers to help out more on my projects. I want my wife and kids to attend to my needs. I want my church to focus its ministries on me. I want the world to feel the gravitational pull toward the center of the universe, which is, of course, my own life. And with all of those sentences, you can easily spot the problem: "I" pops up a lot.

It is a sinful way to live. We use people as service animals in our lives. It translates to using religion to gain comfort and a nice reputation. It culminates in using God as a sacred Santa Claus or a cosmic traffic cop. The demand that everyone around us become our slave means that we have completely lost the scope of God's sovereignty. It becomes the most insidious type of idolatry, where we ascend to God's throne thinking we deserve the service due only to Him.

That is why we must consider servanthood as a spiritual discipline. It is not just being nice to one another. Servanthood is allowing the love of God to motivate our way of life. The demand to be served is the essence of ego and arrogance. Pushing the spiritual discipline away, we lower the worth of others' lives while increasing our own. It is a life devoid of the love that should characterize the Christian. So when we turn our heart toward Jesus and allow affection for Him to rule, then serving like Him becomes our habit. Our service of others becomes an extension of our love for Jesus. Certainly, we serve others because we care about them, but it is a display of our love toward God that can sustain our service toward others.

It is the love of God that compels us to live out the implications of the gospel. As we are transformed by it, we assume the posture of a servant. As with the other habits for our holiness, being a servant requires intentionality. Our natural bent is to be served. To conform our lives to Christ, we must be like our Master who chose to serve. Just as God is love, we seek to live for that love, in that love, and express that love to others.

TWO BOWLS OF WATER

The Bible is filled with juxtapositions. Very often, if you're looking, you can find two objects, people, or events that, when compared, provide a compelling lesson. We find such a scenario at the end of Jesus' life, during His final week of public ministry before the crucifixion. He and the disciples had entered Jerusalem to take part in the Passover Feast, which included a meal that carries much symbolism on its own. An odd thing happened before the night was over. Jesus, the master, would become the disciples' servant.

The Bowl in the Upper Room

The twelve disciples had joined Jesus in an upper room for the Passover supper (Luke 22:7–14). In Middle Eastern culture then (and in many places still today), meals are eaten while reclining at short tables. People lean to one side and prop up on pillows. It results in one person's feet being not so far from another person's head. This being the case, a servant was often assigned the duty to wash the guests' dusty, smelly feet once they entered the home. At this dinner, Jesus took on the role. We don't know if there was no servant present, if no one had washed even their own feet, or if anyone had offered to wash the feet of others. It is reasonable to surmise that everyone simply entered the room, dirty feet and all, and sat down for the meal. So Jesus poured water in a bowl, put a towel around His waist, and began washing feet. At one point, Peter bristled at the idea but Jesus assured him of the necessity for this action (John 13:5–11).

Consider the men whose feet Jesus washed. Judas Iscariot had already come under the power of Satan and would betray Jesus to the executioners. Simon Peter tried to refuse Jesus' act of service and within the next few hours would deny that he even knew Jesus. Thomas was absent so long after Jesus' execution (in fear perhaps) that he would miss the first resurrection appearance and then doubt that it happened. The other nine apostles would all go screaming into the night like scared children when Jesus would be arrested.

They were all utterly confused. How could the Messiah stoop so low? The task of washing feet was for the lowliest of servants in a household. In their minds, Peter was right in his attempt to stop Jesus. But Jesus followed His actions with His teaching.

"Do you know what I have done for you? You call Me Teacher and Lord. This is well said, for I am. So if I, your Lord and Teacher, have washed your feet, you also ought to wash one another's feet. For I have given you an example that you also should do just as I have done for you. I assure you: A slave is not greater than his master, and a messenger is not greater than the one who sent him." (John 13:12b–16)

They needed to see the example of service from Jesus so they would learn that it was a holy privilege instead of a headache. Our Lord left all of us with this example that we should serve one another.

The Bowl before Pilate

Shortly after the Last Supper scene, Jesus is betrayed and arrested. The Jewish leaders drag Jesus from leader to leader and from illegal trial to illegal trial over a twenty-four-hour period. Each political leader wanted nothing to do with the man they simply considered to be a wandering rabbi. He was more of a nuisance to them than a rebel. Finally, Jesus landed in the presence of Pontius Pilate, the governor.

In that day the custom was that the Roman political leader would release a prisoner during the Feast of the Passover. Pilate presented two options for the crowd to pick for release: Jesus the wandering teacher or Barabbas the notorious prisoner. The religious leaders revved up the crowd, and they called for the release of Barabbas. Pilate was likely shocked that the Jewish crowd kept saying of Jesus, "Crucify Him! Crucify Him!" But, for this man of power and authority, I find his next move most shocking.

> When Pilate saw that he was getting nowhere, but that a riot was starting instead, he took some water, washed his hands in front of the crowd, and said, "I am innocent of this man's blood. See to it yourselves!"
>
> All the people answered, "His blood be on us and on our children!" Then he released Barabbas to them. But after

having Jesus flogged, he handed Him over to be crucified. (Matt. 27:24–26)

Where our Lord used a bowl of water to serve, Pilate used a bowl of water to wash his hands of the whole messy Jesus situation.

THE WAY OF PILATE OR JESUS?

It leaves us with a serious decision to make. When things get hard, it is the natural inclination to just wash our hands of others. Those with power and prestige say it is not just acceptable but expected to wash your hands of difficult situations.

People are messy. In fact, they often drag me into their own mess. Taking time for the powerless and the hopeless costs a great deal. In these moments, you must choose the way of Pilate or the way of Jesus.

Who will we imitate? One thing I know: We will always imitate the one we love.

The way to Christlikeness is to get on the floor and wash feet. It is a choice. Servitude reveals a heart ready to be shaped by God. It demands discipline as our flesh fights against it. You and I will make a choice based on either the default position of self-preservation or love for Christ based on the Savior's sacrifice. But if you want to be like Jesus—and you do—then servanthood is the only path to take. As He said in John 13, the

> *The way to Christlikeness is to get on the floor and wash feet.*

156

servants are not greater than the Master. So, it should not be offensive or even an embarrassment to serve as Jesus served. It is where we are not just seeking to know God but, by His grace, to be like Him.

PRACTICING SECRETLY

Most of us are impressed with fame. Thousands of radio and TV stations, magazines, and websites help us pay attention, with daily reports dedicated to what famous people do. In fact, some of the most famous people in the world are famous for simply being famous. Perhaps some have positively influenced the world through charity work, but few have changed the world. But they are beautiful and famous, and for some reason we like to know where they vacationed last week. It is likely an extension of our adolescent need to sit at the cool kids' lunch table. We want to be recognized by everyone. Our hunger for popularity gets in the way of our servanthood.

Once when Jesus was teaching about giving, He said, "But when you give to the poor, don't let your left hand know what your right hand is doing, so that your giving may be in secret. And your Father who sees in secret will reward you" (Matt. 6:3–4). By serving in secret, we concern ourselves with God's affections as our primary relationship. Rather than make a show of it and seek the approval of others, we serve only because of the approval we already have from God.

When we serve, we must do so with only God's heart in mind. If you serve for the purpose of being noticed, celebrated, or rewarded, then you've missed the point altogether. Serving others is another way that we increase in our faith in God and love for God. It is an act of faith because you are committing your energy to another's preservation and care. In faith, you leave your own care in the hands of the Father. Walking away from our approval-addiction, we can more fully enjoy the Father's love.

SERVING THE SPIRITUALLY LOST

Pastor John Ortberg calls servanthood the ministry of the mundane.[1] It is a perspective worth embracing. Most people in your life do not need you to do something earth-shattering. You don't always have to seek out grand designs for world change. Be willing to enter into the everyday needs of common people. Our neighbors simply need compassion. Because of our relationship with Christ, the compassion you possess first originated with God as He shared it in your sufferings. So even in the mundane, we are acting as tools in the hands of God to show spiritual care.

Servanthood is often seen in the willingness to be interrupted. Rather than plow ahead with your personal agenda, service requires you to expend time on someone else. As you choose to minister, it becomes more than the mere declaration that you care about your friends. It is even more than the assertion that you love your friends. The time and energy spent in serving them shows them that the love you profess is real. As we do so, we may have opportunity to tell them that your love stems from the love that the Father has shown you.

Our service should be shaped by that boundless attitude that no interruption is too great when someone else is in need.

Jesus willingly changed His circumstances of existence in

order to serve unlike anything we could imagine. Christ died on the cross in our place for our sins—the greatest act of service, for it restored our relationship with God. It is the ultimate in relationship restoration. Serving one another makes a difference in our relationships here on the earth. Jesus' service created eternal intimacy and community.

We are not winning anyone's salvation, but we are deepening our relationships. Through the simple tasks of changing tires or delivering food, we show esteem and value for one another. Everyone who receives the gift of service from you knows that selflessness is involved. They are not ignorant of the personal cost to you. As you serve, you build up the body of Christ because you reflect the heart of Christ.

SERVING FELLOW CHRISTIANS

Serving one another within the body of Christ means using our spiritual gifts. In 1 Corinthians 12–14, Paul described how we are to use our spiritual gifts. It is here that we learn that the Holy Spirit has empowered us for works of service to build up the church. We use our gifts to express the gospel. But it is also with great intentionality in how we do so. In 12:18 we learn, "But now God has placed each one of the parts in one body just as He wanted." Your acts of service are due to the presence of the Holy Spirit within you. He is directing and empowering you to minister to others. As you minister in His power, it is then for His glory.

The body of Christ imagery drives home for us that through service, we discover the interdependence shared among believers. The church is very much like the sequoia trees in

California. There are more than eight thousand trees in the Giant Forest of Sequoia National Park, and the largest, the General Sherman tree, is one hundred feet in circumference at the base of its trunk.[2] The trees are likely the oldest living organisms on the planet.

It is an overwhelming sensation to be in the presence of a forest of trees that stretch more than two hundred feet into the air. But the most amazing aspect is their root system. One would logically conclude that such enormous trees would have roots that dig deep into the earth. But the opposite is true. Instead, their roots are only five feet deep. But they stretch out sideways through multiple acres of territory. In doing so, the roots intertwine with one another. The way that these massive trees stand up during the storms is by their interdependence. They quite literally hold one another upright.

Believers' service to one another is the same kind of interdependence. We sustain one another through the storms of life. Servanthood is not just being nice. It is lending weight, support, and compassion to another human who is struggling through life's trials. For your brothers and sisters in the kingdom, serving them is not a chore assigned to you by a capricious parent. Serving Christians is fulfilling Galatians 6:2 when it says, "Carry one another's burdens; in this way you will fulfill the law of Christ." Bearing another's weighty load is a work of imitating the divine.

> *Bearing another's weighty load is a work of imitating the divine.*

SERVING THE WORLD TOGETHER

Let's consider a few specific ways you can engage individuals and the church through the discipline of servanthood. The service that Christians can offer the world is a true view of justice. We are not just merely promoting religious ideals and spiritual virtues. You and I can express the heart of God through promoting compassion and justice. In doing so, we are obedient to the Word and building up holiness as a habit.

Remember, servanthood is a choice. Paul wrote, "For you were called to be free, brothers; only don't use this freedom as an opportunity for the flesh, but serve one another through love" (Gal. 5:13). Every time you look at your schedule, you make a choice about what to do with your day. The same is true of your bank account and skill set. In Christ, God has freed you from the power of sin. In our love for Him, we are daily bringing our lives under His lordship. So, as Paul says, our love for one another—and consequently for God—can be expressed through acts of service.

Offer Provision and Hope

And who needs this service? Eventually, everyone. From the cultural elite to the outcast, everyone will need compassionate care along life's journey. But throughout the Bible, God emphasized that His people should care for the marginalized among humanity. Jesus taught us, "Whatever you did for one of the least of these brothers of Mine, you did for Me" (Matt. 25:40). It is a jarring statement. It was to the original hearers and it is to me. When I give food to the homeless, hope to the immigrant, and comfort to the orphan, it is as if I'm personally caring for Jesus the Christ, the Son of the living God. It should revolutionize the way we view servanthood. So let's look at a few ways to live out this discipline of serving people in big and small ways.

Consider the role of justice in the world. It is popular to be an activist. Just watch your social media feed and you'll witness all sorts of calls for the world to change and for people to make a difference. Of course, this is more "hactivism" than activism—just social-media hacks decrying the decay of the world but doing nothing about it. As ambassadors of the one true King, we should dedicate ourselves to the cause of justice. We should take action, but in so doing we should never allow ourselves to fall into the trap of acting without being motivated by Jesus' love for the mistreated. The gospel must be our reason to seek justice on the part of those who are suffering.

Serving means that you are going to stand in the gap and supply someone's needs where they have no way to do it on their own. Think then about the urban poor who are barely surviving or the homeless in your city. What actions can you, your family, and your church take to meet those needs? It can take many forms that keep you at arm's length, but that was never the posture of Jesus. He got involved in the lives of those He touched.

As you find ways to feed, clothe, give shelter to, and educate those in impoverished circumstances, do so with the idea that you will also befriend them. Otherwise, you are simply a baptized version of the governmental agencies that treat people like numbers on a spreadsheet. We are called to love people as we serve them. Filling a pantry with food is a good deed. The church must take it further and share our lives with the poor so they can meet the King.

A more radical way that I'd encourage you to serve your fellow man is through ministries that seek to free people from injustice. In your city, there are women trapped in the "sex industry." It is just a sanitized term for those who work in strip clubs, make a living as prostitutes, or are tragically kept as sex slaves. The church cannot turn a blind eye to sex trafficking. In the world today, there are tens of millions of slaves. We need to be the modern-day abolitionists who are motivated by the gospel's power to liberate the soul and demand for the liberation of the body as well. The trafficking of human beings in our cities and around the world demands for the church to stand up and serve the powerless. With the multitude of ministries that already exist and the gifting that God has placed in your local church, we can serve this woefully underserved oppressed population.

Help the Widow, Orphan, and Immigrant

In the Bible, the poor are normally referenced through the real-life images of the widow, the orphan, and the immigrant (sometimes referred to as "the alien"). Modern-day estimates set the number of orphans worldwide at over 140 million. Widows are likely around you on a daily basis in the grocery store and in your own church family. Every day, throngs of immigrants enter our country with starry-eyed dreams of a better life. If several members in each church in your city decided to become foster parents to children in the foster-care system, we could reduce the size of many foster-care institutions. If each church decided to adopt a widow or widower to care for their needs, none would be hungry or alone. If each church decided to adopt an immigrant people group, we could serve them their daily bread and the Bread of Life. From mundane actions to the mammoth endeavors, we should fulfill the desire of God that His people care for these on the outskirts of culture. The Lord's heart for them is clear, and so should be our hearts.

Assist the Affluent with Their Needs

Servanthood can also take place if you live in an affluent suburb. Many homes there are filled with beautiful decor but the souls of their inhabitants are empty. Just as the cause of the impoverished ghetto needs compassion, so does the suburban wasteland. We have become too good at turning a deaf ear to the alcoholic mom, abusive husband, suicidal teen, and nearly bankrupt family living in our subdivisions. Being a servant means knowing the community and breaking into relationships. I have lived in the suburbs for most of my life. It is the place where courteous gestures are accepted but deep friendships are rare.

When it comes to this culturally acceptable separation with neighbors, we believers can forge a new path that people actually long to enjoy. Their defenses are often on high alert. Yet Christians in communities often turn a deaf ear and cold shoulder to their neighbors. Why? The daily grind of work may put you on edge against people while at home, not wanting to take time or thinking everyone has a selfish agenda. Quite frankly, many people have simply not had a good friend since high school or college. And some neighbors, if you introduce yourself, will be suspicious until they clearly see that you have no personal plan to get them on the Home Owners Association board, host a party to sell your favorite vitamins, or mow your lawn while you go on vacation.

So approach them with an others-centered agenda. They'll probably not know what to do at first. It will be new and unfamiliar territory.

But stay the course. As you combat the superficiality inherent to them and the culture, it will take time and it will be messy. But take comfort in knowing that it is the simple things that often make a great spiritual impact. Cultivate your friendships over what you have in common: the kids' school, sports team, or cooking out on the grill. One of the best things to do is simply invite them over for a meal. Think about it. How many neighbors within a quick walk have invited you into their home? For many, the answer is zero. Be the person who allows *your* home to be a place of rest from the hardships of the world. Once they have cracked open the door of their hearts, then let your neighbors pour out their dreams, hopes, and beliefs regardless of how wayward it all sounds. You will win a hearing from them if you will win their heart first.

> *Cultivate friendships over what you have in common: the kids' school, sports team, or cooking out on the grill.*

Rather than the "Hi. How are you? Just fine. How are you?" sterilized conversations, we probe deeper. Our servanthood should be jarring to the lives of people who are hooked on self-image and self-preservation. As we give away our time and efforts, it will create relational space to talk about the gospel. Service should always lead to evangelism. Evangelism should always lead to service.

A SERVANT'S GREATEST HELP: THE GOSPEL

Ultimately, the greatest way we can serve anyone is with the gospel. In his first letter to the Corinthian church, Paul described the gospel as the "most important" thing for him to tell and them to hear (1 Cor. 15:3). In the gospel we see the service of God toward us. We find freedom from our sin. The God of the universe shows His love for us and we, in turn, give our love to Him. It is in servanthood that we meet Jesus as He dies to turn away the wrath of God from our sin-soaked hearts.

In this new freedom, I am happy to become a servant once again. But now, I am a slave to God and a servant to my fellow man still trapped in sin's death grip. Paul also said of his own ministry, "To the weak I became weak, in order to win the weak. I have become all things to all people, so that I may by every possible means save some. Now I do all this because of the gospel, so I may become a partner in its benefits" (1 Cor. 9:22–23).

Our willingness to serve is a signpost pointing others toward the Messiah. My freedom is of little consequence unless I can love others toward an understanding of Jesus and tell them of my Savior's glorious love.

Chapter 10

TREATY OR SURRENDER:
THE PRACTICE OF SUBMISSION

You are in a war. Yes, a war. The spiritual disciplines engage us in this great spiritual battle. They are the motions we make toward love and holiness. With them, we are working out our salvation in the everyday life of work, relationships, and our devotions with Christ. But make no mistake, the warfare is real.

The war is for the eternal destiny of your soul. As a believer, that outcome has already been determined. Because of God's grace, the moment you put your faith in Christ, victory was the banner flying over you. Our task was not to earn His grace. We simply received it. But now our work is to walk in ongoing obedience to His calling in how we live out the unmerited favor given through Christ. The habits for our holiness give us paths to walk through the minefields of this battle.

The spiritual disciplines focus our minds so the fog of war does not cloud our judgment. They provide us the tools to participate in the great rescue mission for our friends and the global population.

In the first part of this book, we looked at the proverbial "big three" of spiritual disciplines: worship, Bible study, and prayer. They form the bedrock of our habits for holiness. Then, we moved through fasting, fellowship, rest, simplicity, and servanthood to get a view of how we can love God more thoroughly and He can shape our hearts more missionally. Now, in these final few chapters, I want to narrow your focus even more. With the practices of submission, leadership, and disciple-making, we will move quickly through each with a view as to how God is guiding us to think deeply about our loyalties to His sovereignty.

TREATIES AND POWER

Global politics sounds like an ominous phrase. But it is simply the way of the world. Empires rise and fall. Just ask the pharaohs, kings of Europe, and infamous dictators of the twentieth century. However, a few institutions have outlasted all the empires of history. Two such institutions are a treaty and the act of surrender.

When one country makes a treaty with another country, power does not shift. Each country keeps its borders in place. Each remains independent and sovereign. The ruler or ruling body of each country continues their work. But what they do differently is, essentially, trade favors. It could be lending money, open trade agreements, or even helping to defend against other aggressive nations.

SURRENDER AND SUBMISSION

The act of surrender is quite different. When a nation surrenders, its sovereign borders are taken down. Controlling power is given away to another's power structure. Instead of trading favors, every resource is now owned (or a portion is controlled) by the stronger party.

God does not accept treaties. The only acceptable way forward is unconditional surrender. We do not run to the border of our little kingdom and demand that the Creator of the universe respect our boundary markers but trade favors with us. It is ludicrous to think that God will share in our power-hungry desire to rule. He is the King of kings and Lord of lords. There will be no sharing of sovereignty. Why should there be? He is a good King, gracious to His subjects. We, on the other hand, are arrogant, backstabbing, greedy, lustful creatures who love to deceive others to gain the upper hand.

God knows we need a complete transformation, which is impossible to accomplish under our own power. So He offers us life when we surrender to His love, His grace, His mercy, His salvation. That is the nature of submission.

The surrender we make to God is one that is not of terror but love. We see in Him such a love for us—as defeated as we are—that we are compelled to love Him as deeply as we can learn. The treaty would simply keep us at odds with God's kingdom, still fighting for our eternal survival—and that without any hope. The surrender holds the promise of communing with the Lord in an eternal covenant. We are called to and need to submit to His authority.

AS JESUS PRAYED

The garden of Gethsemane is the bookend to the prayer life of Jesus, the final recorded prayer before His walk to Calvary. Remember that at the beginning of His ministry, Jesus fasted forty days and then faced Satan's temptations. Now, as the conclusion of His ministry approaches, He separates Himself from the apostles for a little while to pray before His arrest and crucifixion.

> He fell facedown and prayed, "My Father! If it is possible, let this cup pass from Me. Yet not as I will, but as You will." . . . Again, a second time, He went away and prayed, "My Father, if this cannot pass unless I drink it, Your will be done." (Matt. 26:39, 42)

In the garden prayer, Jesus teaches us two things about submission. First, we learn that it occurs in the context of relationship. Jesus addressed God the Father. It was not an impersonal and passionless portion of the Trinity to whom Jesus spoke. Rather, He was communing with the Father who loves the Son and is pleased with Him. We live out a reality reflecting the same principle. We are not submitting to a nameless, faceless power. Rather, we do this in the context of a loving covenant. We submit because we love Him. He accepts our surrender because He loves us.

The second lesson from the garden prayer is that submission is hard. It is why we should view it as a discipline. In a brief amount of time, the Son asks the Father about the "cup" passing from Him. In other words, Jesus is asking if there is another way to obtain our salvation. Being divine, the Lord knows there is not. I believe His request and immediate submission takes place to give us the example that submission is necessary, even when it is difficult. The gospel of Luke records that Jesus anguished through the prayer and sweat drops like blood (Luke 22:44). It is under this extreme pressure that Jesus entrusts Himself to the will of the Father. Thus, our salvation is won through His death and resurrection.

So our salvation arrives when we surrender to Jesus in faith. Our holiness is developed as we continue to walk in submission to His Spirit. Saint Ignatius once prayed:

> Lord, I freely yield to You all my liberty,
> Take my memory, my intellect, and my entire will.
> You have given me everything I am or have;
> I give it all back to You to stand under Your will alone.
> Your love and Your grace are enough for me,
> I ask for nothing more.[1]

With this prayer, we see a picture for our own abandonment to God. It is the portrait of one laying down the heavy burden of self-rule. Rather than choose our own experiences, intellect, and self-direction, we submit joyfully to live by God's love and grace. Nothing more.

SCENES OF YIELDING CONTROL

King David

King David and the prophet Elisha are two other men in the Scriptures who offer similar examples of relinquishing control. Psalm 51 is a prayer of relinquishment by King David. We traditionally understand it to be his prayer following his great fall into adultery and murder. The king committed adultery with Bathsheba and then sought to deceive her husband Uriah about the circumstances of Bathsheba's pregnancy. When his plan failed, the king gave orders to the military commander to leave Uriah stranded in battle alone so he was consequently killed. But the Lord witnessed David's trail of sins and confronted him through Nathan the prophet. Psalm 51 seems to fall into the life of David at the time of his repentance.

In his prayer to God, King David asks for God to extend grace and to wash away his guilt. Though he sinned against Bathsheba, Uriah, and the nation, David admitted that the chief one he offended was God (v. 4). As he seeks for God to restore the joy of salvation (v. 12), David realizes what God required of him. "You do not want a sacrifice, or I would give it; You are not pleased with a burnt offering. The sacrifice pleasing to God is a broken spirit. God, You will not despise a broken and humbled heart" (vv. 16–17). God did not need the wealth or power under David's control. God wanted David's heart. When David submitted to the Lord again, he was able to receive the later title in Scripture: a man after God's own heart (1 Sam. 13:14; Acts 13:22 NIV).

David's prayer teaches us that we must place our lives under the loving care of God. He does not want our substitute sacrifices or hollow confessions. He wants—and requires—our submission, not our stuff.

The Prophet Elisha

Elisha gives us a second example of submission to the will and work of God. As Elijah's days as Israel's prophet ended, God directed him to lay the mantle of work upon Elisha. At the time, Elisha was minding his own business and running a farm. But, when he realized the new calling that was placed upon him, Elisha took drastic measures. The passage reads, "So he turned back from following him, took the team of oxen, and slaughtered them. With the oxen's wooden yoke and plow, he cooked the meat and gave it to the people, and they ate. Then he left, followed Elijah, and served him" (1 Kings 19:21). Elisha's family must have been in good financial circumstances. Verse 19 records that he was plowing with one of his twelve teams of oxen. In a bid to ensure his own commitment and celebrate his calling, Elisha destroyed any chance for going home. He did not leave a plan B. For him, there was no safety net. Now he would give himself over completely to the will and care of God.

Elisha destroyed his plow and cooked up the oxen for a huge feast. It likely fed much of the community. Elisha walked away from his world's standard of success. Rather than run a large farm, he followed God's calling. We do not read where he took any servants, resources, or even influence with him. Elisha abandoned himself to the care and power of God.

SPURNING SHORTCUTS TO THE LIFE OF FAITH

No Quick Path

These two biblical examples demonstrate why the intensely personal spiritual discipline of submission is necessary. It's in our nature to find the path of least resistance, like rainwaters during a storm. As the waters fall upon the earth, they immediately seek to run downhill. The quickly occurring streams will skirt around obstacles, finding the route of least resistance. Similarly, we look for the life path that holds no problems, causes no delay, and gets us where we want to go without any problems.

We want success quickly and we want it easily. With our religion, we will take shortcuts to get a good reputation. Our hearts will deceive us into thinking that the easy way is the best way. But, in fact, the life of faith is difficult. Thus, we need to submit ourselves to "the author and perfecter of [our] faith" (Heb. 12:2 NASB). God's plan for our salvation required the hard path of sacrifice and death of His Son. David's path was one of humble confession and repentance. Elisha's path was one of "no turning back." Ours should be no different. Empowered by the Spirit, you can relinquish your future into the caring hands of God.

Confession Required

Submission is a disciplined action also because it requires a confessional spirit. The confession of Jesus was not about sin, as He had committed none. Instead, it is a confession in the broader sense of the word: agreement. He agreed to follow the Father's will. Even in the agony of the physical moment, Jesus yielded to what would happen next under God's perfect plan. David's confession in Psalm 51 falls into the more narrow understanding of acknowledging sin. He agreed with God on the rebelliousness of his actions. Submission requires disciplining our hearts and minds to agree with God in all things. It is a loving surrendering to the Lord's will and standard for holiness.

Elisha's confession was not with words but with deeds.

Understanding the assignment given by God, He submitted to the calling. Submission, in this sense, is embracing God's plan rather than continuously putting forth our own. Without doubt, you and I have a plan for life. Some of us may have a plan for domination: We wake up each morning deciding how we will rage against the machine, stick it to the man, grab the bull by the horns, and be the masters of our own fate. The better choice would be to humble ourselves before the Lord and allow His calling to rule our lives.

A War against Our Ego

All of this is a war against pride. The spiritual discipline of submission reigns in our ego. With it, we declare that there is a better ruler for our lives. Rather than the prodigal nature lurking in our hearts, we are happy to choose Jesus. Submission is done either because you are forced to do so or because you desire to do so. There is no middle ground.

The Bible tells us that at the judgment seat, every person in history will bend the knee and confess the lordship of Jesus. For the believer, we've already done so not because of judgment but because of salvation. Now, every time I submit to God's plan, will, and Spirit at work in me, I do so because of love. I love God. I love how He loves me. I love the ways He chooses to use me in His rescue mission. A life of relinquishment to the Creator is not only wise, it is wonderful.

> *A life of relinquishment to the Creator is not only wise, it is wonderful.*

SURRENDERED TOGETHER

With such an intensely personal discipline as submission, it is tempting to say that we must practice this discipline alone. But believing friends can assist us in at least one way. It is with the practice of accountability. Paul refers to it in his letter to the Ephesian church:

> And don't get drunk with wine, which leads to reckless actions, but be filled with the Spirit: speaking to one another in psalms, hymns, and spiritual songs, singing and making music from your heart to the Lord, giving thanks always for everything to God the Father in the name of our Lord Jesus Christ, *submitting to one another in the fear of Christ.* (Eph. 5:18–21, emphasis added)

Though you'll read more of the practical actions of submission in the two final chapters, just consider its personal implications now.

God calls us to surrender to Him. In doing so, He connects us to the church. The Bible describes the church with several images: a family, house, building, body, royal priesthood, adopted children, and heirs of the promise. In many of these descriptions and others in the New Testament, the church is presented as a group of people related to one another. In healthy relationships, there is accountability. It is how we practice submission together. Rather than trying to go alone, we go together. For us to go together into the grand work of God, we must not just rely on each other but protect one another. With accountability, I submit to the loving heart of the church that will call me home when I wander away.

In Galatians 2, Paul records that he opposed Simon Peter publicly (2:11–14). Peter was separating himself from Gentile believers when Jewish believers came near. Paul held Peter accountable to the truth and for his sinful favoritism. Today our relationships should be the same. When you see a fellow Christian allowing sin to abide in their life, you go to the person in love. You hold up the standard of the gospel and ask them to live according to it. The call to repent is perceived by the world as mean-spirited and narrow-minded. The call to repent is known by Christians as the loving act that brings us back to the peace of the gospel.

We practice this discipline by trusting in the love that the church has for us. Will the church fail us? It has in history and can do so in our own lives. But it is through the church that God is at work in the world. It is in the community of faith that we learn how to apply the Scriptures to real-life scenarios. As older believers instruct less mature Christians, we are held accountable to live in holiness. As younger believers run headlong into the adventurous gospel mission, older believers are challenged to never allow apathy to creep into their souls. The surrender we make to one another is a signpost of our surrender to the one Lord over us all.

THE MISSION OF SUBMISSION

Arrogance, pride, and self-determination are hallmarks of this world. As a result, many think submission, relinquishment, and surrender are what losers do. So when you and the church practice submission, you are reflecting an ethic that the

177

lost will thoroughly question. As with the other disciplines, this is exactly the response we *want* from those who are perishing. We want them to ask *"Why?"*

Submission works its way through many of the other disciplines. It will make servanthood possible when it is inconvenient. When the world is going to the lake while you're attending worship, it is a witness that you are committed to honoring God. Your mention of times of Bible study, prayer, and fasting will evoke questions about how you spend your time. Daring to take time to rest rather than work your fingers to the bone evokes curiosity out of those who are tired from the demanding pace of life. In all of these ways that we place ourselves under the lordship of Christ, the lost will want to know why.

Rather than hide our loyalties, we tell them about the One we love. Don't give in to the politically correct rhetoric that tells us to obscure our religious views from the public. Instead, declare your love for Jesus by openly discussing how He has a will for each person. Perhaps you can tell how Christian friends have called you back from the brink of disaster by holding you accountable. It is not a burden to bear but a joy that uplifts.

In many ways, we live out the mission of God by simply giving credit where credit is due. It may be in a quiet conversation or in a major public forum. When the Golden State Warriors won the National Basketball Association championship, few had thought they could win it all. They won the title by beating the Cleveland Cavaliers and its star player, LeBron James. In the post-game interviews, numerous members of the Warriors spoke about their Christian faith. It is not an uncommon occurrence among professional athletes who are Christians. Many led off with thanks to God for His blessings, and then thanked their teammates, coaches, spouses, and the rest.

Among the Warriors, Andre Iguodala (the Finals most valuable player) mentioned the faith that was palpable among the team. He thanked the chaplains that served the NBA teams. Of his teammate Stephen Curry, that season's MVP, Andre said, "I want to be just like Steph when I grow up—just a God-fearing man."

Here were two men at the top of their (literal) game. They were the champions and faith was a natural subject. It is a lesson for all of us. Being 5 feet 8 inches, I'll never play in the NBA. I'm not going to make it as a movie star, and the world stage will likely never take note of me. But my neighbors will. My coworkers are watching me because I've told them of my faith in Jesus.

As we surrender to His will, we can become showpieces of His grace. At every turn when success happens, we can give Him credit and let others ask why we don't take it for ourselves. That is the heart of submission before a holy and great God.

Submission is not about being subhuman or loathing ourselves. It is finding our true worth in the relationship forged by the cross and empty tomb. In your daily discipline of relinquishing power to Jesus and living with the accountability of friends in the faith, you will find love. It is the love that dies for you and gives all for your holiness.

Chapter 11

TRAVELING TOGETHER:

THE PRACTICE OF SPIRITUAL LEADERSHIP

L eadership is present in every arena of life. We find it in the
high-rise offices of the global cities where economies rise
and fall. It also appears on every playground when one kid says
to the others, "Come on. Let's go play tag. I'll be 'It' first."

Not all leadership, however, is good leadership. Certainly
most is not spiritual leadership. That is why I classify spiritual
leadership as a discipline for Christians to develop.

Earlier in the book, we noted that the world defines success in terms of power, money, and achievements. These three
factors are seen so clearly in how we choose leaders. Think of
entrepreneur Donald Trump, who became the surprisingly
popular 2016 candidate for president. With power, money, and
achievements typically running the show, Christians should
quickly embrace why a change is needed. Think through the logical outcome if these three factors control how and why we lead.

Many political and military leaders of history amassed power and influence. Machiavelli, Julius Caesar, Attila the Hun, Napoleon, Mussolini, and Mao Zedong (transliterated Mao Tse-tung) are just some of the names that come to the forefront. The last one was influenced by the writings of Sun Tzu, a Chinese general whose ancient work *The Art of War* about warfare tactics remains influential in twenty-first-century America today. Sadly, many in business and church leadership have read this book over the last decade as if it is a textbook for leadership. Sun Tzu wrote, "The consummate leader cultivates the moral law, and strictly adheres to method and discipline; thus it is in his power to control success."[1] He focused on the control of processes rather than on any needs of the people the ruler led. Niccolo Machiavelli, in portraying the prince who longed for zero rivals in the kingdom, wrote, "It is better to be feared than loved, if you cannot be both."[2] It stands as a caution to use the influence we have carefully.

Wall Street was a hit movie from the 1980s. In it the fictional character Gordon Gekko (played by Michael Douglas) said the following:

> The point is, ladies and gentlemen, that greed—for lack of a better word—is good. Greed is right. Greed works. Greed clarifies, cuts through, and captures the essence of the evolutionary spirit. Greed, in all of its forms—greed for life, for money, for love, knowledge—has marked the upward surge of mankind.

Many have pointed to these lines as emblematic of the greedy decade of the 1980s. I would point to them as clearly unveiling our own hearts. Greed still marks the surge of mankind—the *downward* surge. Getting more is the whole point of the leadership of many. Roger Starr, who once worked in the New York Planning Office, said, "Money is the most egalitarian force in society. It confers power on whoever holds it."[3] Holding the reins of financial power gives one the sense that they control the world around them. It deludes us to reality.

Achieving success through our projects is the endgame of many people's attempt at leadership. One anonymous quip states, "Success comes to the person who does today what you were thinking about doing tomorrow." Leaders value decisiveness and action points that lead to completion of projects. Never mind if the projects added great value to individuals or the human race. The mere achievement stands as its own symbol of success, no matter how hollow it might truly be.

The faulty premises on which leadership naturally occurs in the world—and in our hearts—is why we must view spiritual leadership as a discipline. Remove the idea of holiness and love for God from leadership and all you have left is selfish dictatorial impulses from the human heart. When leadership is defined by our love for God and the desire for holiness, then gospel-motivated sacrifice takes center stage. It transforms how we understand the way God leads us. Our love for Him can grow deeper as He empowers us through the Holy Spirit to lead others toward that very same love, transforming our fleshly desires to be in line with God's holy character.

LEADING RELATIONSHIPS

What Is Missional Leadership?

Leadership is a discipline because it demands effort and focus. But it also is a discipline because it requires effort in our relationships. When you remove relationships from your work of leadership, you are left with a brutal dictatorship. As we think about leadership from this new perspective, we must consistently keep in mind how leadership is formed in our life by our relationship to God and how that in turn informs one's relationships with the people around us.

A few years ago I completed doctoral studies. The subject of my doctoral project was combining the words and then defining the term "missional leadership." Look at any book-buying website and you'll find more titles on leadership than you could ever hope to consume. Searching Amazon.com for "leadership books" brings up 24,672 results. Searching for "spiritual leadership" yields more than 17,000 results. It is a popular subject. As I've thought about how we should lead as believers, I developed a biblically based and Christ-centered definition for missional leadership:

Missional leadership is living according to and speaking comprehensively about the mission of God as first revealed in the Scriptures and the life of Jesus Christ so as to guide others to surrender to and participate in the mission of God on a personal and community level.

Exploring the Definition

Breaking down the definition into its various phrases will help us understand how leadership is a discipline that we work out in our relationships.

Leadership begins with "living according to and speaking comprehensively." Leadership is not just a mental exercise of being the smartest person in the room. It's also not simply imposing your will on people. It must begin with devoting your own life to God's work, which results in having your words consistently honor Him in guiding people toward God's work as well.

Missional leadership continues when we live and speak about the right thing; namely, "about the mission of God." If we lead for our own pleasure, ego, or cleverness, then we miss the point. The leadership that leads to holiness is what guides people toward God's redemptive work.

> *The leadership that leads to holiness is what guides people toward God's redemptive work.*

When we lead people in God's mission, we must do so from the authority as it is "first revealed in the Scriptures and the life of Jesus Christ." Even as spiritual people, however, we are tempted to define God's mission in our terms. We find good things to do and good things for the church to do. Instead, we must let the Bible and the life of Jesus be the authority of how we live and where we lead others.

When we lead it must be "to guide others to surrender to and participate in the mission of God." The discipline of leadership must be centered on how others can better relate to God. Leading people through legalistic hoops will create moral people. Leading people to academic excellence will produce smart people. Leading people to engage in social justice will give us compassionate people. But there is a better way. It is the best way: Leading people to surrender to God will create holy people.

As you fall deeply in love with God, then it will be natural to lead others to do the same. The discipline you will need involves guiding your friends (both old and new) toward God Himself, rather than the effects of a relationship with Him. As you help people follow Him, then He will help them fulfill His mission.

Finally, as is obvious by now, missional leadership happens "on a personal and community level." Your current role in life might be for influencing one or just a few people. Embrace it! The relationships you have are precious, as each individual has an eternal destiny. In leading that one person, you are pointing him or her toward the God who loves beyond measure and away from the hollow promises of the enemy. Value every level of leadership you are given whether it is for a family, small group of friends, church body, or an entire community.

LEADERSHIP AS A GIFT

As you can clearly see, leadership never happens in a vacuum. It can be argued that there is a type of self-leadership, but the real sense of the concept is that leadership is a gift placed into the lives of God's people to influence both the Christian and the one who is yet to believe. God gives leadership roles for spiritual purposes. To better understand it, let's look at an Old Testament story.

First Samuel 2 reveals that Eli was the priest at Shiloh and a judge for Israel. The Lord had assigned a critical role of leadership to him. As was the custom, his family would follow in his role of priesthood and leadership. Sadly, his sons did poorly at the work. They were morally corrupt men who had no regard for God or for the worshipers (vv. 12–13). Eli's sons, Hophni and Phineas, would pilfer from the meat that was brought as a sacrifice to God. It was so offensive to God that He declared to Eli that both his sons would die on the same day as a sign of the Lord's judgment (v. 34).

But then the Lord gave a word of hope for the people who would need a leader. God said, "Then I will raise up a faithful priest for Myself. He will do whatever is in My heart and mind. I will establish a lasting dynasty for him, and he will walk before My anointed one for all time" (v. 35).

God Raises Leaders

In this verse we find core ideas about how leadership is formed by God in such a way that it drives us to holiness and draws people into His work. The first is that God is the One who raises up leaders. We must submit to His choosing. But it is hard. We are enamored with the good-looking, well-spoken, and well-educated. In other words, we want Saul to be the king. Sadly, once "that guy" is the king, his ego often overtakes his faithfulness. Instead, we must be willing for God to choose a shepherd boy like David instead of the popular guy like Saul.

Leadership is a role that is often sought after. It is not evil to desire leadership. Paul wrote, "This saying is trustworthy: 'If anyone aspires to be an overseer, he desires a noble work'" (1 Tim. 3:1). The key is that we must discipline ourselves to see leadership as noble work on behalf of others rather than a way to seek self-fulfillment. Our leadership must come from God calling us out rather than selfishly seizing power. To live in such a way, we must love God supremely. It is why Jesus described our relationship with the vine and branches metaphor in John 15. Recognizing that He is the source of life, our desire is to simply abide with Him. As He then directs, we will lead, serve, guide, follow, or whatever action God gives us.

Leaders First Serve God

The first duty of leadership is to serve God and His mission. By first turning our hearts toward God, then priorities will be set in their proper order. It does not mean that we will exclude others from the process. But walking before God's "anointed one" (in 1 Samuel, a foreshadowing of the Messiah) is the primary task. This idea does set leadership in an upside-down manner for us. We think of leadership as guiding humans. But in His declaration to Eli, the Lord says that the leader He raises up will be "for Myself."

That seems odd to us because God does not need someone to lead Him. It is why we need a clearer understanding of leadership. Our work is not simply to steer people like spiritual traffic cops. *We serve God, and by our example of word and deed, God gives direction to people.* The deeper your love for God, the more effective your leadership for others. Our worship, ministry, and life of holiness for God will be translated into leadership for others.

Leaders Direct with Discernment

The leadership that God demands of us must be comprehensive. The Lord told Eli that the new leader would serve according to the heart and mind of God. Spiritual leadership is birthed from God, not from our own cleverness. We learn to lead with discernment because God has no interest in aimless wanderings. He has a mission to be fulfilled. By our digging into the study of Scripture and prayer, God will give us His mind on the issues of our day. But we also need His heart. A smart person with zero compassion makes a great professor. Conversely, a compassionate person with little knowledge makes a comforting friend. Neither is the leader we need for the work of God's kingdom. Rather, we need God's insight and His passion for kingdom glory to be alive in people. Those consumed with God's heart and mind will find leadership becoming a natural outflow of His work.

Leaders Desire a Legacy for God

The final detail to see from God's statement to Eli is about longevity. Leaders are people who should be consumed with the moment and concerned about a legacy. God planned to give this newly raised leader a "lasting dynasty." Our leadership can be short-lived due to selfishness or have eternal consequences because it is Christ-centered. It depends on where you put your eyes. Human leadership concerns itself with the moment's success and satisfying an audience. Missional leadership values the eternal implications of God's glory displayed so that people can experience His redemptive work.

BIBLICAL MOTIVATIONS FOR LEADERSHIP

The human condition pushes against all these ideas. Our deceitful hearts don't long after eternity or God's glory. Remember, we want to amass power, hoard possessions, and achieve success in projects. Our bent is to value self-promotion over surrender. Recognizing our nature is another lesson in why holiness is more than just positive morality. The habits for our holiness are God's tools to make us into the people who are separated for His purposes. In contrast, the world demands a smash-and-grab style of leadership. This style has no place in the life of the Christian or the church. We have three much better motivations to lead when called out by God.

First, we are motivated by the very idea of the kingdom of God. The church is the kingdom force on the earth that heralds the King and His kingdom. It is an inaugurated kingdom that is present and still arriving. Everything in the created order and in eternity is under the sovereign rule of God. But there are still rebels. So we lead because God is the true Ruler and we love serving Him. He is a kind King and cares for the people of His kingdom. The church does ministry because we are a sign and an instrument of God's kingdom in the world.

Second, we should be motivated by the covenant of God. A covenant is when two parties make promises to care for one another. The covenant that we have with God through Christ is our promise of redemption. We lead because we are led. Our life is secure in this covenant of grace. Because of it, God's Spirit resides in us to teach us who He is and how we are to live. The covenant is one of love, not legalism. As we love God with our whole heart, mind, and strength, we will lead others who also can become part of the covenant. It is not exclusive to a few saints roaming the earth. It is available to all.

Third, we lead because of the mission we have been given. Jesus prayed, "I am in them and You are in Me. May they be made completely one, so the world may know You have sent Me and have loved them as You have loved Me" (John 17:23).

The mission of Jesus is to unite people into one redemptive family under the redeeming love of God. It is not about a political coup, although He rules over all earthly powers. It is not to demand all the financial resources of the world, although He owns it all anyway. It is not about proving how much can be achieved, although He can do more as an afterthought than we can with all of our might. Ultimately, the mission is about people. It is the rescue of the lost to make them the saved, to make the sinner into a saint and the outcast into a family member.

As God calls you to lead in the church, among friends, in a family, for the community, at work, and in the world, do so for the people. Processes are necessary but they are not the mission. Missional leadership is by its nature outwardly focused on how others can fall deeply in love with the Messiah.

PRACTICAL LEADERSHIP

All of these models and motivations must be worked out in the real world. It must happen in the context of our own lives and how we live with others. After all, if you are leading but no one is following, then you're just out for a lonely walk. So learning how to lead is part of the discipline of helping people move into God's agenda for their lives. Here are a few practical ideas about how to get going in spiritual leadership.

Develop Character

Above all, start with yourself. Leadership without character is tyranny. The Bible never gives us a "command and control" military-style leadership structure for the church. Rather, we witness Jesus Himself submitting to the Father's will. We watch as the apostles grow in their understanding of the gospel and applying it into their own lives. For example, Simon Peter learned by observing Jesus minister to others and eventually by being confronted by Paul (Gal. 2:11–14) for his hypocrisy when Peter tried to hide his friendship with Gentiles. If Peter, a pillar of the early church, needed to grow, so do we. As we're learning, our character will develop only as much as we closely associate with Jesus. Give Him your love and He will give you His character.

Pray

By the world's standards, stopping to pray seems a waste of time. For some leaders, it is a display of passiveness by those too cowardly to make a decision and act on it. But we know differently. Through prayer our faith is enlarged, our minds are informed by God's Word, and our hearts are filled with the Holy Spirit. Leaders pray because they are utterly dependent upon God to go ahead of them in every arena of life. Prayer keeps the spiritual leader from running headlong into a mistaken mission. Instead, in prayer, the Spirit guides us as to how we can act redemptively and live compassionately toward those outside the faith.

Prayer is also an act of leadership that we take with other people. Leaders in the world are pressing followers into action. Leaders in the church should have an even greater impulse of pressing friends into communing with the Father. It is not to move action out of the picture but it is so that we can help our friends see the value of relationship over activity. Missional leaders guide people to prayer, and through prayer experience the covenantal relationship with Christ.

Often we think of the term "leader" in a technical sense—someone with a title and an official capacity in the church structure. But every one of us has influence among others. Parents lead children. Husbands and wives influence one

Prayer keeps the spiritual leader from running headlong into a mistaken mission.

another. Siblings, coworkers, classmates, and friends can all lead each other in this arena of life. Remember, you and I are leaders. We make the critical choice each day of pushing people to just be busy or leading them into the eternity-altering relationship with Jesus.

Give Wholehearted Effort

To lead, there must be a direction we take and actions we make. So after forming character by a strong relationship with God, it's time to go. In moving people into God's mission, it must not be with a halfhearted effort. Leadership is fulfilling but it takes exertion. God's call for you into leadership is not that you'll attempt to use all of your energy but that you commit all of your life. By doing so, you'll both help believers know what to do and show a witness to unbelievers about what God can do.

Look around and you'll see people giving all of their energy to all sorts of pursuits. Hobbies, work, sports, money, popularity, fame, power—these things can consume our lives. As coworkers ask you about your life, days away from the office, and how you spend your free time, God gives you the open door to share about why your faith takes center stage. Your testimony of leading a children's Bible study group, raising support to end human slavery, or caring for widows at a local assisted living home will show that you have a different view of life. As they seek to understand why you would be so selfless, you can lead them to the One you serve.

Be Among the People

Leadership, in the final assessment, must be lived out practically among people. Now, I know that sounds elementary. But the word "among" is what we need to dwell on. It is how Peter described the work of pastors. "Shepherd God's flock among you" (1 Peter 5:2). He was telling the leaders of the church to care for those God had entrusted to them. It is not about leading a charge from so far out front they can barely see you. It is also not driving them from behind because you are frustrated with their lack of progress. Ministry leaders get into the middle of the mess of everyone's lives and lead them like close, personal friends. If you try to drive people like cattle, you'll likely get trampled by an angry herd.

This is the way of Jesus. He came in the incarnational mission to save us. While here, He lived among us. "The Word became flesh and took up residence among us" (John 1:14). Eugene Peterson paraphrases that verse as "The Word became flesh and blood, and moved into the neighborhood" (THE MESSAGE). Leadership takes more than being the smartest or boldest person in the room. It takes love. It is a love that can only be learned and gifted to us by Christ.

In *The Two Towers,* part of the Lord of the Rings trilogy,

J. R. R. Tolkien described our Christ well in the character of the powerful White Rider: "The Dark Lord has Nine. But we have One, mightier than they: the White Rider. He has passed through the fire and the abyss, and they shall fear him. We will go where he leads."[4]

In the story, an evil one was seeking to destroy the beauty of the land, Middle Earth. But a leader stronger than death itself had arrived to be their hero. Grab on to this idea. The Christ, the Son of the living God, is your hero. He has shown us the perfect example of love and service. His leadership is by the power of His holy character and He wants you to know Him in a redemptive covenant. If you will choose to lead others by the way of holiness, you'll never have to fear the dark. The earth will still be grim and life will still be filled with difficulties, but you as a missional leader will always have the Light alive in your soul.

Chapter 12

CITY MISSIONARIES:
THE PRACTICE OF DISCIPLE-MAKING

S ome memories stay at the forefront of your mind. Often these memories are associated with major changes in your life. The moment the sanctuary doors swung open and my bride walked down the aisle for our wedding ceremony is always with me. The first time I looked at my sons when they were born is unbelievably clear. It is my hope that we can all have spiritual experiences that are indelibly secured in our minds.

When my father knelt with me beside the sofa in our living room and I became a Christian is quite clear even to this day. The sense that God was calling me into the ministry at the age of fifteen was thrilling and terrifying all at once. As a memory, it is a constant companion. But there are other significant spiritual moments as well. For me, they have to do with how others worked in my life to make me a better disciple and how God used me to aid others along the way as well.

One such moment was a conversation with my friend

Matthew Roskam. He was the guy who discipled me after I surrendered to vocational ministry. He helped me to better understand the holiness of God and how to live out my faith. I also remember the moment that Matthew essentially graduated me from our discipling relationship. It was short and simple. After I finished preaching at a large church, he walked up, shook my hand, and said, "Now . . . we're just friends."

Then there are the moments when I sensed God using me in the life of another person. In college, I led Bible studies on campus on the idea of practicing our holiness. Angie and I sat with our sons to witness the moments that they became Christians. As a church planter, I sat in a coffee shop, listening to people connect faith with the rest of life. Even more vividly is the moment that a friend who struggled with belief came to place his trust in Christ. These are the moments I hope will not just be remembered, but repeated.

Within such activities abides the core of our faith. Aiding a friend mature in Christ makes clear to us God's love, and it reminds us of His pure love for us. As the love of God drives our lives, then we are growing in holiness—the goal of each spiritual discipline. In these moments, we are fulfilling His will to be missionaries to our cities. As a result, we engage in the discipline of making disciples.

DISCIPLE-MAKING: THE FINAL SPIRITUAL DISCIPLINE

Disciple-making may not have been on your list when you thought about the spiritual disciplines. But I believe it properly fits here. The disciplines are a way we express our deep love for Christ—and experience His deep love for us. What better act of love can we show for Him than to seek that the whole world—beginning with the people right around us—follows Him with the same kind of love? It is also our demonstration of love for the other people walking the planet. We see them as the image-bearers of God but marred by sin's weight upon them. A love for God drives us to have the whole world love Him as we do. A love for others drives us to see them redeemed by the One who can bring transformation.

Making disciples has the greatest of eternal implications. It is the call, work, and lifestyle of leading others to follow Christ just as we have committed to follow Him. The work of making disciples includes everything from befriending unbelievers and sharing the truth of the gospel, to guiding people to obey the commands of the Bible. Interestingly, every Christian is responsible to do disciple-making. Nowhere in the Scriptures are we told to wait until we've grown a certain amount or gained certain knowledge. Rather, as disciples, we are to work toward producing other disciples.

It is the place where many of the other disciplines converge upon one another. It is the work that requires speaking the Word, prayer, serving others, leading, and various other acts of love.

Making disciples also deepens our own relationship with Jesus. Helping others to see the beauty of a covenant relationship with Jesus becomes a constant reminder to us of what we enjoy. And in discipling we are living out the words of Paul from 2 Corinthians, having God make His appeal through our lives (5:20). Developing habits of holiness in new disciples draws us closer to Christ, because we must initiate the habits personally in order to lead in them publicly.

IN PLAIN SIGHT

Making disciples is a spiritual activity. We engage in disciple-making not as professors seeking to educate sinners, nor as legalists hoping to simply moralize the world. Instead, in heeding one of Jesus' last commands to us, we are calling others to follow Him as the Lord of their lives.

Making disciples is also a discipline. In order to follow Christ's command, we must be intentional and single-minded.

We need discipline to live in such a way. The intentional choices for the spiritual over the flesh must be constant. Why? Our hearts produce idols. They seek safety and comfort. If it's hard, we avoid it. We have a hurry sickness because we hide our discomfort in the plain sight of over-activity. Involving ourselves with the stuff of earth is easier than tackling the issues of eternity. We sit behind digital screens and build up a following on social media because it's like a game to play. Meanwhile, we are called to be in the world, in the lives of people in order to reveal the mystery of Christ to them. We hide in plain sight when instead our faith should be on display.

It is why I've written this book: to view the spiritual disciplines as something for us, for others, and for the world. It was undoubtedly God's intention to save you by His redemptive mission. But that's not all! The mission of God included your salvation but it did not end with it. You have the hope of Christ in you and you're growing in it. Now it is time to share it with the world.

After His resurrection, Jesus gave us the Great Commission. He said:

All authority has been given to Me in heaven and on earth.
Go, therefore, and make disciples of all nations, baptizing
them in the name of the Father and of the Son and of the
Holy Spirit, teaching them to observe everything I have
commanded you. And remember, I am with you always, to
the end of the age. (Matt. 28:18–20)

GOING PUBLIC WITH OUR FAITH

His command means that we are to go public with our faith.
The love you have for God needs to be visible. No hiding. No ob-
scuring. It is the evidence of a transformed life. You have been
made holy, different, and set apart for God and His purposes.

For some reason, though, we get sweaty palms and tongue-
tied when it comes to being evangelistic. We often simply
engage in "drive-by witnessing." We are not to randomly confront people, however, shove a gospel tract in their hands, and
hope for the best. Yet when we treat evangelism haphazardly,
that is what we do. Witnessing becomes a mechanical, checklist, get-it-done behavior. It removes a love for God and a love
for others from our lives. Treating disciple-making as a spiritual discipline places it back in God's hands as an action He
does through us. Take a look again at how Jesus described it.

First, Christ gave us the bookends around the commission. He started by saying that all authority in all of eternity
belongs to Him. Then He ended by saying not to worry because
we would always have Him with us. When you and I go public
with the gospel, we never go alone. The Spirit of Christ indwells
us. He will guide our thoughts and words to say what is biblical.
He will enrage your heart against the devastating effects of sin

in others' lives. He will cause you to have joy as you obediently embark on the ministry of delivering the gospel.

It is the beauty of this discipline—as with all of the others—that we do these things by being fueled with the grace of Jesus. Our holiness is dependent upon His presence. Enjoying His work through us in such moments can only increase our love for Him.

Between these two assurances, Jesus gave the command to "go . . . and make disciples." The Greek verb tense used in the verse means "as you are going." Though you may have a specific place that God sends you on mission, all along the way we do this work. Some may feel a burden for a specific ministry. Perhaps you sense God drawing you to minister to widows or immigrants or a people group in another country. It could be that your place is working with your peers in the same stage of life.

If you have such a burden, read this clearly: Do it. Go all in with it. As you do it, though, never miss an opportunity to repeat the same holy gospel ministry with someone "not in your target group." Our work is done all along the way of life. Just because you are great working with English-as-a-second-language groups does not give you a pass on witnessing to your neighbor who grew up here. We call people to Jesus in every occasion.

Jesus gave us a specific thing to do. It is not the work of making religious adherents or good church members. We make disciples. Working in the lives of friends, we guide, persuade, teach, warn, and lift up the beauty of the Christ before them. Sometimes it will happen in an instant. Many times it will be a long relational journey. But regardless of the time frame, we are in the work of making people into lifelong followers of Jesus. Our great mission in life is to help other people trust in the Messiah and start living by His power. We are on the rescue mission to see God release people from the power of sin and live in His righteousness.

The temptation, again, will be to make good religious people. But Jesus is not looking for people who merely go to church or who know about the Bible and religious ideas but don't know Him. Nor is He trying to make your friends into morally superior beings because they tried hard. Embrace the fact that your friends and the people around the world are spiritually dead. They are facing an eternal sentence of judgment for their sin. Our work is to lead them to the infinitely merciful God and say, "Follow Him!" We don't make legalists, mystics, or champions for social justice. We make disciples. Because we know the love of God and hold a love for God, we make disciples who can have the same experience.

Each new disciple must then take the next two natural steps of obedience. First, we guide them to be baptized. The act of baptism does not hold a magical power to it. Rather, it is the public declaration of a once-dead person that they are now alive by the work of God. It is an act of a person saying to the world, "I belong to God and I am one of His people." They are telling the world that they deeply love this God who deeply loves them.

The second step of obedience is "teaching them to observe everything I have commanded you." Teaching disciples to obey God's commands is not a small thing. To be a disciple maker, you are in it for the long haul with this new believer. Teaching them who Christ is, watching them place their faith in Him, and then walking with them toward maturity is how a disciple maker lives. Plus, the emphasis is that we teach them *everything* Jesus commands.

Disciple-making requires love for the person you are discipling. It is the only way that you will stick it out with them. During their journey toward maturity, they will falter, just as we have. As they grow, temptations will turn into sin and they will need your loving admonishing. The disciple will have a lack of understanding that you will fill with scriptural wisdom. And, like us, they will be rebellious. Love will help you persevere during the tough moments of the discipling relationship and magnify the victories of it.

RIGHTS AND FREEDOMS

The discipline of making disciples will take you to a new level of discipleship in your own life. By its nature, holiness requires that you are set aside for God's specified purposes. To do so means that you set aside your perceived rights in life. Growing up in one's faith means giving up the childish need to have it my own way.

Of course, you have the political right to not care. It is your social right to defend your liberties to say what you want to say, do what you want to do, and go where you want to go. But God has given you a spiritual freedom that ought to supersede all of these pitiful worldly rights. Freed from such cares, you are liberated to call people into a new kingdom that is breaking into this world. The Christ who wept over Jerusalem (Luke 19:41) reframes our view of the world. Rather than a place to dominate, it is a place to demonstrate the gospel. All of the spiritual disciplines lead to this place. With love for God taking center stage, we want all men to know Him. With our love for men so overwhelming, we want them to be saved by God.

In the time when Jeremiah was a prophet, many of the Israelites were living in exile. While away from their homeland, they had to make a choice of how to live. Would they create little subcultures in which to exist attempting to be untouched by the rest of the world? Or would they do something about the world in which they now lived? Through Jeremiah, the Lord gave them an unmistakable direction. "Build houses and live in them. Plant gardens and eat their produce. . . . Multiply there; do not decrease. Seek the welfare of the city I have deported you to. Pray to the Lord on its behalf, for when it has prosperity, you will prosper" (Jer. 29:5–7). The will of God was for them to work for the good of those who were not yet of the faith. The people of God were to settle into this place and "seek the welfare of the city." Rather than hide like reclusive monks and nuns, they were to engage the people and openly live out their faith.

Our calling as Christians is no different. We need to passionately seek the welfare of the people in our city. Reframe your outlook on the place where you live so that being a missionary is the normal way of life. We must do so even when we face those who actively oppose the gospel. Jude told the early believers, "But you, dear friends, as you build yourselves up in your most holy faith and pray in the Holy Spirit, keep yourselves in the love of God, expecting the mercy of our Lord Jesus Christ for eternal life. Have mercy on those who doubt; save others by snatching them from the fire; have mercy on others but with fear, hating even the garment defiled by the flesh" (Jude 20–23). When you face the doubter, have mercy. When you see those who are in danger, snatch them from the fire they do not even know burns so close. Go into your city with the weeping nature of Jesus that desires for sin to die and for the spiritually dead to live.

YOUR NEW HABIT

The only way that you and I will live this way is by making holiness habitual. Our habits are formed by default and by choice. We stumble into some habits just by the force of life. I drive in certain lanes on the interstate in certain spots because I've done it so often. I do it to find the path of least resistance. I tell my wife "I love you" repeatedly because it's true and I never want her to sense a hesitation in my heart—not even for a moment. The default position of people is to rebel. The new discipline we need is to love God with all of our heart, soul, mind, and strength. Through the gospel, we are freed to be the people who will live in such a way. It will require that you—as a disciple maker—lead them in a better way.

It is time for you to live out the spiritual disciplines with love as the centerpiece and mission as the result. Along the journey, you will grow up in Christ and grow closer to your friends in the faith. Always remember that the habits of your holiness should arise from an inward love for Christ. Your faith that is intensely personal will be mirrored by a faith that is boldly public. When we love Him supremely, we will gain the desire to draw people toward Him. The calling to live on God's mission locally and globally will become the normal way of life. With love as the center of the spiritual disciplines, we will mature spiritually, gather people for deeper relationships, and live on mission with boldness.

AFTERWORD

A s you finish this journey through the spiritual disciplines, here are a few parting thoughts.

First, let me say a sincere thanks for joining me in considering these habits for our holiness. For many of us, considering such changes in our lives is daunting. I appreciate that you would trust me through all of these chapters to point you toward Jesus.

Second, we all need a warning. The spiritual disciplines are tools in the hands of God. But they must never be allowed to overshadow Him. In Numbers 21, the Hebrews were in the wilderness wanderings and complaining again. God punished them by allowing poisonous snakes to enter the camp and bite them. As many began to die from the venom, others begged Moses to intercede before the Lord, and he did. God told Moses to make a snake out of bronze and hang it high on a pole. Anyone who looked to the snake—as an expression of faith—would live (vv. 5–9). It was an Old Testament foreshadowing of Christ being hung on the cross.

About four hundred years later, after many years of inhabiting the Promised Land, the people again were deep in sin. But when Hezekiah became king, he sought to cleanse the land of its idolatry (2 Kings 18:1–4). He tore down the idols and places of false worship, and he broke into pieces something he called Nehushtan (v. 4). It was the bronze snake. For centuries, the Hebrews had kept the bronze serpent. Now it had become an idol to worship.

We need this warning. You and I must never let the tool that God uses become the object of our worship. The spiritual disciplines can help you, but they cannot save you. Spiritual disciplines are paths on which we walk, not treasures to which we cling. Make sure to focus solely on the Lord and not on what you can accomplish. Practicing the disciplines can make you appear moral. But if practiced without laying your affections on Christ, they will rot your soul with legalism. Continually keep His call before you to "love the Lord your God with all your heart, soul, mind, and strength."

Third, with that warning in mind, keep going! In the disciplines, we learn that grace cannot be earned but that effort can be empowered. It is God's desire that you grow in your affections toward Him and faith in His mission for you.

I hope that this journey through the disciplines has informed your mind and inflamed your passions. Now it is time to put down the book and take up your life in Christ. This will require you to be disciplined, and we will all need help. The disciplines are practiced better when we encourage one another. If you have not already done so, decide right now which one of the disciplines will aid you most in expressing your love for Christ and start there today.

Finally, it is time to tell others about this journey. As you've found these new arenas of Christian life helpful, tell someone else. Invite them to study these disciplines so they too can better express their love for Christ. I would love to hear from you as well. Through the various social media accounts and sites, please let me know how these disciplines are impacting your walk with Jesus. I'd love to know that you are growing in your habits of holiness. You can contact me at Twitter: @philipnation, Facebook: philipnation, or at my personal website philipnation.net.

I pray that the Lord will bless you with a deep and abiding relationship with Him. May He drive His Word deep in your heart and propel you far into His mission. For all of us, let's love Christ supremely, talk about the gospel comprehensively, and care for our neighbor completely.

NOTES

Introduction: A New Look at Old Practices

1. William Law, *A Serious Call to a Devout and Holy* Life, ed. John W. Meister and others (Philadelphia: Westminster Press, 1955), 27.

Chapter 1: Travels through the Garden: Coming to Love Christ

1. Said by Mr. Beaver in *The Lion, the Witch, and the Wardrobe*. Aslan is the great lion and true ruler of the land of Narnia. Lewis uses Aslan as a figure for Christ throughout The Chronicles of Narnia.
2. Songwriter and author Michael Card uses the term "fragile stone" to describe Peter in his book and compact disc by the same name. See Michael Card, *A Fragile Stone: The Emotional Life of Simon Peter* (Downers Grove, IL: InterVarsity, 2007).
3. O. Palmer Robertson, *Christ and the Covenants* (Phillipsburg, NJ: Presbyterian and Reformed Publishing House, 1980), 4.
4. Thomas Merton, *Comtemplative Prayer* (New York: Doubleday, 1969), 37.

Chapter 2: Our Soul's Desire and Design: The Practice of Worship

1. William Temple, *The Hope of a New World* (London: Epworth Press, 1953), 7.
2. Dallas Willard, *The Spirit of the Disciplines* (1988, repr. New York: HarperCollins, 1991), 177.
3. Peter Kreeft. *Prayer: The Great Conversation* (San Francisco: Ignatius Press, 1985), 70.
4. C. S. Lewis, *Letters to Malcolm* (1963, repr. New York: Harcourt, 1992), 89.
5. Brother Lawrence, *The Practice of the Presence of God and Spiritual Maxims* (New York: Dover Publications, 2005), 10. The book is an

unabridged publication of *The Practice of the Presence of God the Best Rule of Holy Life, being Conversations and Letters of Nicholas Herman of Lorraine* [Brother Lawrence] (New York: Fleming H. Revell, 1895) and *The Spiritual Maxims of Brother Lawrence* (Philadelphia: Griffith and Rowland Press, n.d.).

Chapter 6: A Partying People: The Practice of Fellowship

1. C. S. Lewis, *The Weight of Glory* (New York: HarperCollins, 1976), 46.

Chapter 7: Driving in the Slow Lane: The Practice of Rest

1. Henri J. W. Nouwen, *The Way of the Heart* (New York: Ballantine, 1981), 17.

Chapter 8: Possessing Possessions: The Practice of Simple Living

1. Adapted from Merrill F. Unger, *Unger's Bible Dictionary* (Chicago: Moody, 1957), 413.
2. Rob Berger, "Top 100 Money Quotes," *Forbes*, April 30, 2014. Berger features Rogers's memorable quotation at the top of his list. See http://www.forbes.com/sites/robertberger/2014/04/30/top-100-money-quotes-of-all-time/

Chapter 9: The Ministry of the Mundane: The Practice of Servanthood

1. John Ortberg. *The Life You've Always Wanted: Spiritual Disciplines for Ordinary People* (Grand Rapids: Zondervan, 1997), 97, 100.
2. The General Sherman Tree http://www.nps.gov/seki/learn/nature/sherman.htm.

Chapter 10: Treaty or Surrender: The Practice of Submission

1. As quoted in Peter Kreeft, *Prayer: The Great Conversation* (San Francisco: Ignatius, 1985), 172.

Chapter 11: Traveling Together: The Practice of Spiritual Leadership

1. Wu Tzu, *The Art of War*, IV. 16., as quoted in David G. Jones, *The School of Sun Tzu: Winning Empires Without War* (Bloomington, IN: iUniverse, 2012), 123.
2. Niccolo Machiavelli, *The Prince and Other Writings*, trans. W. K. Marriott (New York: Fall River Press, 2008), 80.
3. *Money and Wealth: A Book of Quotations*, ed. Joslyn Pine (Mineola, NY: Dover Publications, 2013), 182.
4. J. R. R. Tolkien, *The Two Towers* (New York: Ballantine, 1954), 110.

Join Philip as
the journey continues.

Check out his regular posts at **www.PhilipNation.net**

**Engage in the conversation with Philip about
how we live out our faith on topics like:**

Spiritual disciplines
Missional living
Leadership
Culture
Discipleship
(With some fun along the way!)

Find out more about Philip, where he is speaking, and how you
can have Philip speak for your church or organization.

(